Type your username and password or register by clicking on **Create a new account**.

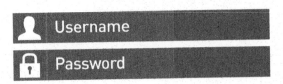

👤 **Username**

🔒 **Password**

In MyBook you can access the accompanying resources (both text and multimedia), the **BookRoom**, the **EasyBook** app and your purchased books.

CODE

❯ JQ36ZPCSum

Type the code in the **Activation Code** field

MY PURCHASED BOOKS

ENTER YOUR CODE   Activation code [   ] ❯

The code must be typed only the fi st time you access **MyBook** and cannot be used thereafter.

APPLIED MACHINE LEARNING
WITH PYTHON

Andrea Giussani

Copyright © 2019, EGEA S.p.A.
Via Salasco, 5 - 20136 Milano
Tel. 02/5836.5751 – Fax 02/5836.5753
egea.edizioni@unibocconi.it - www.egeaonline.it

First international edition: March 2020

ISBN Domestic Edition 978-88-99902-65-0
ISBN International Edition 978-88-31322-04-1
ISBN Pdf International Edition 978-88-31322-14-0

Contents

List of Figures   ix

Preface   xiii

1   Introduction to Machine Learning   1
    1.1   A simple supervised model: Nearest Neighbor   2
          1.1.1   Tuning Hyperparameters with Cross-Validation   9
    1.2   Preprocessing   14
          1.2.1   Scaling Data   15
          1.2.2   Forcing Data to be Gaussian: an Introduction to Power Trans-
                  formations   19
          1.2.3   Dealing with Categorical Variables   21
          1.2.4   Handling with Missing Values   24
    1.3   Methods for Dealing with Imbalanced Data   26
          1.3.1   Random Oversampling of the Majority Class   28
          1.3.2   Random Undersampling of the Majority Class   29
          1.3.3   Oversampling using Synthetic Data: SMOTE   30
    1.4   Reducing Dimensionality: Principal Component Analysis   31
          1.4.1   PCA as dimensionality reduction   32
          1.4.2   Feature extraction   36
          1.4.3   Nonlinear Manifold Algorithm: t-SNE   37

2   Linear Models for Machine Learning   41
    2.1   Linear Regression   42
    2.2   Shrinkage Methods   44
          2.2.1   Ridge Regression   44
          2.2.2   Lasso Regression   49
          2.2.3   Elastic Net   51

2.3   Robust Regression   52

    2.3.1   Huber Regression   53

    2.3.2   RANSAC   56

2.4   Logistic Regression   58

    2.4.1   Why Logistic Regression is Linear?   59

    2.4.2   Logistic Regression Predictions (Raw Model Output) vs Probabilities (Sigmoid Output)   60

    2.4.3   Logistic Regression in Python   61

    2.4.4   Model Performance Evaluation   62

    2.4.5   Regularization   66

2.5   Linear Support Vector Machine   68

2.6   Beyond Linearity: Kernelized Models   73

    2.6.1   Into the Hood of the Kernel Trick   76

    2.6.2   Practical Classification Example: Face Recognition   77

3   Beyond Linearity: Ensemble Methods for ML   83

3.1   Introduction   83

3.2   Ensemble Methods   84

    3.2.1   Boostrap Aggregation   88

    3.2.2   Out-of-Bag Estimation   90

3.3   Random Forests   91

    3.3.1   Random Forests Classifier   91

    3.3.2   Random Forests Regressor   94

3.4   Boosting Methods   95

    3.4.1   AdaBoost   95

    3.4.2   Gradient Boosting   96

    3.4.3   Extreme Gradient Boosting (XGBoost)   99

    3.4.4   CatBoost   106

4   An Introduction to Modern ML Techniques   115

4.1   Introduction to Natural language Processing   115

    4.1.1   Preprocessing with Text Data   116

    4.1.2   Numerical Representation of Documents: the Bag-of-Words . .   121

    4.1.3   Practical Example: Sentiment Analysis with IMDb Reviews Dataset   124

    4.1.4   Term Frequency-Inverse Document Frequency   126

    4.1.5   Bag-of-Words with More Than One Word (n-Grams)   127

4.1.6   Beyond Bag-of-words: Word Embeddings 132

4.2   Introduction to Deep Learning   140

4.2.1   Dealing with Complex Data into a Neural Network 143

4.2.2   Multiclass classification   147

Appendices   **151**

A   A crash course in Python   **153**

A.1   Building Blocks in Python 153

A.1.1   Variables 153

A.1.2   Methods 155

A.2   Data Structure in Python 156

A.2.1   List and Tuples 156

A.2.2   Sets 158

A.2.3   Dictionaries 158

A.3   Loops in Python 159

A.3.1   The For Loop 159

A.3.2   The While Loop 160

A.4   Advanced Data Structure in Python   161

A.4.1   List comprehensions 161

A.4.2   Lambda Functions   163

A.5   Advanced Concepts on Functions 164

A.5.1   The magic of Wildcards into Function's arguments   164

A.5.2   Local vs Global Scope in Functions 168

A.6   Introduction to Object-Oriented Programming   169

A.6.1   Objects, Classes and Attributes 170

A.6.2   Subclasses and Inheritance   172

B   Mathematics behind the skip-gram model   **175**

List of Figures

1.1   Figure 1.1: Training observations, labelled by the target variable.   4
1.2   Figure 1.2: Classification of the test points based on a simple Nearest
      Neighbour.   5
1.3   Figure 1.3: Confusion Matrix on the test Set   6
1.4   Figure 1.4: Sensitivity analysis on the accuracy for different number
      of Neighbors.   8
1.5   Figure 1.5: Representation of a 5-folds cross-validation. This was
      taken from the 11
1.6   Figure 1.6: Principal Component Analysis: Scatter Plot of the Original
      Data 33
1.7   Figure 1.7: Transformation and Dimensionality reduction on a simple
      2-dim feature space. 34
1.8   Figure 1.8: Transformation of the two Principal Components after
      Scaling. 34
1.9   Figure 1.9: Impact of each feature on the first two Principal Components. 35
1.10 Figure 1.10: Application of t-SNE on the digits dataset. 40

2.1   Figure 2.1: Shrinkage effect on the Regression Coefficients in the
      Boston House Dataset under a $\mathcal{L}_2$-penalty model. 47
2.2   Figure 2.2: Mean Training vs Mean Test score under the Ridge Model
      for different value of α, with corresponding uncertainty. We see that
      the uncertanty drammatically reduce its effect after certain values of α,
      and that the train and test looks very similar, though the train always
      performs better than the test set, for those values. 49
2.3   Figure 2.3: Shrinkage effect on the Regression Coefficients using a
      Lasso Penalization. 50
2.4   Figure 2.4: Feature Importance in Lasso regression. 51

2.5   Figure 2.5 Empirical rule in action: outliers notably are identified as
       extreme events in this distribution.   53
2.6   Figure 2.6: Different behaviour of the Squared vs Huber Loss for in-
       creasing values in the model prediction residuals.   55
2.7   Figure 2.7: Fitting of a standard OLS and Huber Regression in the
       presence of outliers.   56
2.8   Figure 2.8: Huber vs RANSAC Regression (under the OLS baseline). .   58
2.9   Figure 2.9: Theoretical Logistic Function, with threshold set to 0.5 . . .   60
2.10   Figure 2.10: Confusion Matrix for the Diabetes Dataset on the Test set.   64
2.11   Figure 2.11: Precision-Recall Curve on the Diabetes Dataset.   65
2.12   Figure 2.12: The Receiver operating characteristic (ROC) Curve   66
2.13   Figure 2.13: Plots of common Classification Loss Functions: on the y-
       axis, we have the loss, whereas on the x-axis we have the raw-model
       output.   69
2.14   Figure 2.14: Scatter Plot of the toy data used for the illustration of the
       SVM.   71
2.15   Figure 2.15: Identification of the Decision Boundaries and Support
       Vectors.   72
2.16   Figure 2.16: Scatter Plot of a overlapping, two-classes, dataset.   73
2.17   Figure 2.17: Effect on the regularization on the margins.   74
2.18   Figure 2.18: A Linear Hyperplane with non-linear data is not feasible. .   74
2.19   Figure 2.19: Fitting a SVM to non-linear data using the Kernel Trick
       produces non-linear decision boundaries.   76
2.20   Figure 2.20: Predicted sample names. Incorrect labels are shown in red.   79
2.21   Figure 2.21: Model Performance on the Face Dataset using PCA and
       SVM together.   81

3.1   Figure 3.1: Feature (global) importance obtained by fitting a random
       Forest Classifier on the Heart Disease Dataset.   92
3.2   Figure 3.2: The role of pruning in control overfitting.   93
3.3   Figure 3.3: Feature global importance in Gradient Boosting Classifier. .   98
3.4   Figure 3.4: Raw SHAP Score for the fourth observation, with the (neg-
       ative and positive) effect of some features explained. Note that in
       red we have features that move positively away from the baseline,
       whereas in blue the ones which affect negatively this pattern.   101
3.5   Figure 3.5: Feature global importance as the average of the SHAP
       value magnitudes across the dataset.   104

3.6   Figure 3.6: Feature Importance for all the dataset units. 105

3.7   Figure 3.7: Dependence Plot for the feature *MaxHR*. 106

3.8   Figure 3.8: Exploratory Data Analysis on the Titanic Dataset. 108

3.9   Figure 3.9: Global Feature Importance on the Training Titanic Dataset
       on fitting the catboost Classifier. 111

3.10 Figure 3.10: Confusion Matrix on the Titanic Test Set. 112

4.1   Figure 4.1: Clusters of selected words, based on their similarity re-
       trived by the Word2Vec model. 137

4.2   Figure 4.2: Representation of a Neural Network Architecture with two
       hidden layers. 140

4.3   Figure 4.3: A linear separable dataset for Classification. 142

4.4   Figure 4.4: Loss vs Accuracy in Fitting a one-layer NN to a linear sep-
       arable dataset. 144

4.5   Figure 4.5: Decision Boundaries after fitting a one-layer NN on a linear
       separable dataset. 144

4.6   Figure 4.6: Fitting a Logistic Regression on such data would lead to an
       inconsistent estimator. 145

4.7   Figure 4.7: Loss vs Accuracy by a one-layer neural network (for dif-
       ferent epochs) on a non-linear dataset 146

4.8   Figure 4.8: Decision boundaries after having fitted a dense neural net-
       work with three layers. 147

4.9   Figure 4.9: Scatter Plot of data concerning a three-class classification
       problem. 148

4.10 Figure 4.10: Decision Boundaries on a three-class problem produced
       by a dense neural network. 150

4.11 Figure 4.11: Confusion Matrix for a three-class classification problem
       produced by a dense neural network. 150

Preface

> . . . the objective of statistical methods is the reduction of data. A quantity of data...is to be replaced by relatively few quantities which shall adequately represent...the relevant information contained in the original data. Since the number of independent facts supplied in the data is usually far greater than the number of facts sought, much of the information supplied by an actual sample is irrelevant. It is the object of the statistical process employed in the reduction of data to exclude this irrelevant information, and to isolate the whole of the relevant information contained in the data.
>
> R.A. Fisher (1922)

These words by one of the greatest Statistician, Sir R.A. Fisher, speak by themselves. I would say, this sentence contains the essence of machine learning, although many things have changed from the last century. For instance, nowadays we typically face datasets where the number of observations is far greater than the set of distinct features. At those times, probably the biggest dataset on which Fisher was working was the Iris dataset, but nowadays we deal with datasets of millions of examples, and therefore all classical theoretical results would, trivially, be satisfied (e.g. the Central Limit Theorem is one of those). On the other hand, in many modern applications, we still have problems of dimensionality, and therefore those words are essentially still very important in the Machine Learning community. With different words, Andrew Ng, Computer Scientist at Stanford University, has recently came up with this sentence:

> Coming up with features is difficult, time-consuming, requires expert knowledge. *Applied machine learning* is basically feature engineering.

In my personal interpretation, featuring engineering is the modern concept of dimensionality reduction, because both of them aim at producing feature extraction to improve the performances of the model. But honestly it would be very reductive to comprise the term Machine Learning to dimensionality reduction.

Machine Learning has gained a remarkable popularity in the last decade, not just because of the massive amount of available data, which is produced by ourself in everyday simple actions, but also because there is a wide consensus that learning from data leads to take better decisions and generate a better understanding of the phenomenon under investigation.

In its very general terms, Machine Learning (ML) can be understood as the set of algorithms and mathematical models that allow a system to autonomously perform a specific task, providing model-related scores and measures to evaluate its performances. It is sometimes confused with predictive (numerical) analytics, which is indeed part of ML, but more related to statistical learning. The range of applications of Machine Learning methods is vast and heterogeneous, from image recognition to topic detection in text analysis, from predicting whether a patient will suffer from breast cancer to predicting the price of a stock in three months from now.

The main objective of Machine Learning consists of predicting an outcome based on a set of features. The model is trained on a set of data, in which the target variable is available, and a predictor (or learner) is obtained. This learner is then used to predict the outcome on new data, that are not available at the time of training, and typically a good predictor is the one that accurately predicts the target variable.

This pipeline describes a discriminative *supervised learning* method, where we aim to predict a (continuous) target variable y based on some features $\mathbf{X}$. In this book, we will focus on *Shrinkage* estimators, *Support Vector Machine* algorithms, *Ensemble* methods and their applications to structured and unstructured data. However, in many applications, we could be just interested in finding some relationship between the target and the features: this is what *unsupervised learning* methods do. Although we will give more attention to supervised techniques, a great deal of attention will be given to techniques for dimensionality reduction, such as the *Principal Component Analysis*, which is a method that basically rotates the dataset in such a way that the rotated features are statistically uncorrelated.

The aim of this book is to introduce the reader to the main modern algorithms, employed by practitioners, to tackle Machine Learning problems, ranging from linear models to modern methods that easily deal with non-linear relationships.

The book has been thought for a broad, not strictly technical audience: on the one hand, the book was proposed for Bocconi Unviersity students, who actually come from applied sciences, and most likely want to learn modern ML techniques to develop modern applications into Economics, Finance, Social and Political Sciences; on the other hand, I strongly believe this book can be a very good pocket-friend for all who wants to use machine learning in their data science and analytics tasks. Indeed, the book is proposed as a sort of cookbook, where each statistical model is presented, and the corresponding code section is provided to consistently apply those concepts to real problem.

I have intentionally avoided mathematics in most places because I believe it is (sometimes) a good distractor from the main objective of this manuscript, that is to empower the beginner learner with machine learning methods. Similarly, in many parts of this book, we have favored exposition over succinctness. I am aware of the fact that most of the code presented here could be tightened up, but that was rationally choosen to illustrate the methodologies to a broad target audience.

Hence, this manuscript was designed and written to be primarily used for practitioners, without the need of going into the math of the algorithms, although I strongly encourange to deepen those concepts with the reading of technical books and specific papers. If you are interested in the mathematics behind the proposed algorithms, there exists many books concerning technical aspects, which are mentioned throughout this book.

The key fact about this book is that it guides the reader into different methods, ranging from Bagging to the modern XGBoost, which is probably the first-best choice for any practitioner in machine learning. This is actually a strong point of this book: to the best of my knowledge, no book has been written giving particular attention to recent ensemble methods, such as XGBoost or CatBoost.

Python is the high-level language on which the analysis are carried out: this is indeed the modern language of applied Machine Learning, and notably modern softwares and techniques are developed in this language. Note that Python is an open-source software, and can be downloaded at the following link: https://www.python.org. I would say, it democratizes the coding era by allowing anyone to produce, promote and mantain a software easily and efficiently. Furthermore, I believe that once learned, it will be much more easier to follow the machine learning community on its developments and improvements.

The book is structured as follows: In Chapter 1, we will describe the standard pipeline that a machine learning algorithm follows: we will cover standard preprocessing and more advanced techniques, such as PCA for dimensionality reduction, and try to understand the fundamental relationship between bias and variance in ML. All the techniques are shown with practical examples. In Chapter 2, the reader will be introduced to a crucial concept in ML, which is the one of shrinkage. This is very useful when we have to deal with many features, such as in genetics, and techniques such as Ridge and Lasso are shown. Furthermore, we will distinguish between classification and regression techniques, introducing firstly the Logistic Regression model and then the Support Vector Machine, which are two classifiers employed when data is linearly separable. A great deal of attention will also be given to non-linear SVM.

In Chapter 3 we will cover one of the the most popular ML techniques, that is ensemble methods, ranging from Random Forest to Gradient Boosting, with different applications. We will cover the XGBoost algorithm, which is the holy grail for any Machine Learner, and a great discussion is also given to SHAP values, which are a great tool to explain any model outputs to a non-technical audience. In Chapter 4 we will speak about two of the main areas where ML can be further investigated: Natural Language Processing and Deep Learning. Both are very hot topics, and the community is continuously working hard to improve the available models. We will just introduce those topics, so I strongly suggest the interest reader to deepen his knowledge with the given references. Since this book is aimed at reaching the broadest audience, I have also added in Appendix A a crash course in Python: this is aimed at not just covering the basics, since it will also introduce the reader to more broad concepts, that necessarily one has to deal with when working with machine learning models, such as Object-Oriented Programming.

Note that this book comes with an online version available at https://mybook.egeaonline.it/login. The online version cannot be downloaded, but it is a colour version to promote code readability. To facilitate the use of the proposed methods, and to improve the readability, I decided to create a book-specific library, called egeaML, which is publicly available on GitHub at https://github.com/andreagiussani/Applied_Machine_Learning_with_Python.

Please follow the instructions available in the GitHub repository to install it. Please, do note that the user can directly install it in any notebook environment, such as jupyter or colab, by simply typing and running the following snippet code:

```
!pip install git+https://github.com/andreagiussani/Applied_Machine_Learning_with_Python.git
```

The ! operator tells the notebook this is not a Python code, but a command line script. The datasets used within the book have been made easily accessible within the repository. Furthermore, the Git repository will be updated periodically with extra material and new notebooks, so I strongly suggest the reader to check it frequently.

Acknowledgments

I would like to thank many people who have helped me in writing this book. Most of them has given support and motivation to continue this project, some of them has given instead interesting insights and suggestions, and this project would never have seen the conclusion without the help of each of them. Among many, I would like to thank Alberto Clerici, who was the first one extremely interested in this project, and who helped me in setting up the final version of this book. I am also grateful to Marco Bonetti, whose interest for statistical learning methods has greatly helped me to improve myself daily, and this has definitely ameliorated the manuscript. I would also thank Egea for having given to me the possibility to write this manuscript with extreme flexibility, and also for the support on the formulation and preparation of this book. Finally, I am also grateful to many colleagues and friends, with who I have discussed this project and gave to me important insights: among them, I would like to thank Alberto Arrigoni, with who I have had nice chats on this fascinating topic, and Giorgio Conte, who has helped me in structuring the GitHub project.

Chapter 1

Introduction to Machine Learning

Generally speaking, when we deal with classical machine learning problems, we typically distinguish between supervised and unsupervised learning methods. In supervised learning, we have a sequence of independent and identical distributed examples $(x_i, y_i) \sim p(x, y)$, where $x_i \in \mathbb{R}^p$ describes a vector of features summarizing the available data, and $y_i \in \mathbb{R}$ is the target variable, that is the dependent variable of our model. The objective of supervised learning is to find a function $f(\cdot)$ so that $f(x_i) = y_i$, that is we need to find a function that approximate the distribution well on the training set but it also generalizes to new, unseen samples that are drawn from the same distribution. This is the real objective of supervised learning methods: based on a labelled dataset, you would like to classify a new data point that comes from the same distribution $p(x, y)$.

On the contrary, unsupervised methods find applications to dataset where the target is either missing or has not been labelled. Such techniques are used to search for common patterns within the available data, since they are characterized only by a vector of input data. Note that unsupervised methods are widely used in many applications: from clustering to topic detection in Natural Language Processing and dimensionality reduction, which is a very wide family of techniques that in this book will be covered in its essential aspects: just to frame the problem, it maps a set of high dimensional input instances into a lower dimensional space, while preserving certain properties of the dataset. Nowadays, dimensionality reduction techniques are also used in many scientifics fields, such as genetics or computer science, where datasets are characterized by a large amount of features, so that we can reduce the dimensionality of the problem while retaining the intrinsic variability of the model.

1.1   A simple supervised model: Nearest Neighbor

Let's introduce the main machine learning modeling pipeline with a simple algo-rithm: the so-called Nearest Neighbors . We will illustrate this algorithm with a clas-sification task, on a 2-dimensional vector of features, but please do note that it can also be used for classical regression tasks. Along this book, we will mainly use scikit-learn. The scikit project started in 2011 (see Pedregosa et al. (2011) for further refer-ences), and it is nowadays the one of the main Python open source platform for machine learning. In the last few years, Tensorflow, developed by Google in 2015 (see Abadi et al. (2015) for details) has gained a remarkable popularity, especially in the Deep Learning community, and is nowadays extensively used to perform ML projects and pipelines.

As a fisrt task, we import the necessary libraries and modules that will be used in this Chapter.

```
In [1]: from egeaML import *
        from sklearn.model_selection import train_test_split
        from sklearn.model_selection import cross_val_score
        from sklearn.neighbors import KNeighborsClassifier
        from sklearn.metrics import confusion_matrix
        from sklearn.preprocessing import scale
        import pickle
```

Using TensorFlow backend.

```
In [2]: import warnings
        warnings.filterwarnings('ignore')
```

We import and read the data, which is available in the GitHub repository, as follows:

```
In [3]: reader = DataIngestion(df='data_intro.csv', col_target='male')
        data = reader.load_data()
        X = reader.features()
        y = reader.target()
```

Note that the data have been read using the egeaML specific class DataIngestion, which basically performs the following steps:

1. It reads the data from a .csv file;

2. It split the data into features and target, denoted respectively by X and y.

This set of data consists of only two measurments, that is height and weight, and a target variable, which is the gender of the observed example. Let's recall the main objective of supervised learning methods: we want to train a model, on a specified set of labelled data, and then evaluate its performance on unseen data by comparing the performance of the predicted labels with the available information, typically obtained retrospectively. To evaluate a ML model, what we typically do is to split our data into two set, the training and the test set. This has a major advantage: we can actually train our model on a slice of data, and the rest is then used to evaluate the performance of the choosen model on a set of data that were not used before. While the former is used to build and train the classifier, the latter is used as a holdout set that stands in for future unseen data. This is an important aspect of preprocessing and can be summarized in a very simple rule: do not use any test example in the training phase. Hence, test and training must be kept independent from each other. To do this, we use the scikit-learn method train_test_split from the model_selection module, which requires the user to specify the percentage of the available data to be used for the test set.

The following snippet produce a 2-dimensional plot showing the relationship between height and weight, marked by their corresponding label, which is shown in the Figure 1.1. This was produced using the egeaML method training_class from the class classification_plots. It basically performs the following steps:

1. It takes as input the set of features and the target;

2. It splits the available data into training and test set according to the test size specified as argument;

3. It plots a a 2-dim training set, and each point is labelled by the class it belongs to.

In [4]: `classification_plots.training_class(X,y,test_size=0.3)`

This plot shows the relationship between the two-dimensional, real-valued training dataset, and that there are two classes by which it is possible to split the data. As a consequence, the objective is to split the dataset by gender given two features, weight and height. Nearrest Neighbors works in a pretty simple way: it basically solves the following problem:

$$f(x_i) = y_i \quad \text{s.t.} \quad \text{argmin}_j ||x_j - x||$$

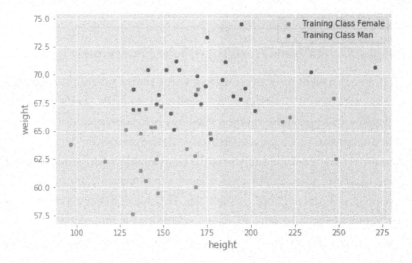

Figure 1.1: Training observations, labelled by the target variable.

that is in order to classify a new data point, we will look, among all the labelled data point, for the closest one, and assign the same training label to the new data point.

A natural question that might arise is: given a set of data, how do we properly train a ML model? How can we try to evaluate the generalization performance of the algorithm we are using? A typical strategy is to split the available dataset into training and test set. Notably, we typically train our algorithm using 80% of the data, and the remaining 20% as the test set. As already mentioned, the two datasets should remain independent, in the sense that none of the examples devoted to the test set should be used in the training phase. For any machine learning model, we also expect that the model should (on average) performs as good as the training phase whenever we evaluate the model on new data. Let's see how Nearest Neighbors works in practice, using the standard scikit pipeline.

```
In [5]: X_train,X_test,y_train,y_test = train_test_split(X,y,
                          test_size=0.3, random_state=42)
        knn = KNeighborsClassifier(n_neighbors=1)
        knn.fit(X_train,y_train)
        y_pred = knn.predict(X_test)
        score = knn.score(X_test,y_test)
        print("accuracy: {:.4f}".format(score))

Out[5]: accuracy: 0.8571
```

We firstly initialize the class KNeighborsClassifier by specifying the number of neighbors, that is the number of training points we want to make the comparison with the one in test: if it is set to one, than the comparison is made with the point which is the closest to the test point. We then fit the classifier on the training set, and then make predictions on the test, calling the scikit-learn predict method. This methods looks for the closest point, and assign its label to the new point.

To evaluate the performance of our classifier, we call the scikit-learn score method, which computes the number of correctly classified samples, and it requires two arguments: the test data and the corresponding labels. We see that our classifier performs well on approximately 86% of the test samples, which is extremely good for such a simple model. We now plot the predicted labels, using the egeaML library, highlighting the ones who were uncorrectly classified by our model:

```
In [6]: classification_plots.plotting_prediction(X_train,X_test,
                                                  y_train,y_test,nn=1)
```

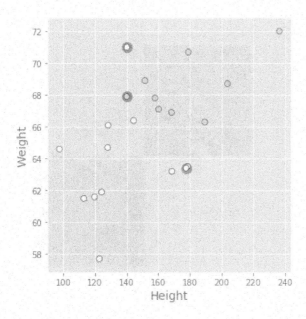

Figure 1.2: Classification of the test points based on a simple Nearest Neighbour.

Remark. *In many situation, we train a model with tons of examples. This translates into a hard worload for the machine, both in terms of RAM and CPU. Training a model does not come for free, so it is good practice to store the fitted model into a pickle file, so that it can be* *called back whenever we like. A possible use of a pickle is to keep track of the fitted model as soon as a new retraining happens. The following snippet shows how to save the fitted knn model into a pickle file.*

```
In [7]: pkl_filename = "my_first_ML_model.pkl"
        with open(pkl_filename, 'wb') as file:
            pickle.dump(knn, file)
```

Another way of evaluating how good we are doing in the test set is with a *confusion matrix*, which diagonal elements represent the true negative (TN) - that is examples that have been predicted as female and are indeed female - and true positive (TP) - that is examples who are men and the model predicted them as men -, respectively. We will investigate different measures of performance in classification tasks in Chapter 2: for the moment, take into account that the model performs well if the number of TN and TP is maximized. The result is shown in Figure 1.3.

```
In [8]: classification_plots.confusion_matrix(y_test,y_pred)
```

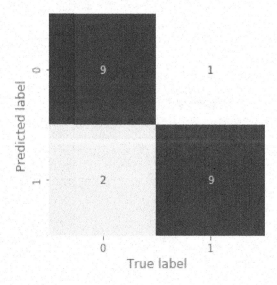

Figure 1.3: Confusion Matrix on the test Set

Please, note that since this function is going to be used throughout the book, if you don't remember the arguments or their position, you can simply employ the help functionality, as follows:

```
In [9]: help(classification_plots.confusion_matrix)
```

Help on function confusion_matrix in module egeaML:

```
confusion_matrix(y_test, y_pred, cmap, xticklabels=None, yticklabels=None)
    This function generates a confusion matrix, which is used as a
    summary to evaluate a Classification predictor.
    The arguments are:
    - y_test: the true labels;
    - y_pred: the predicted labels;
    - cmap: it is the palette used to color the confusion matrix.
            The available options are:
            - cmap="YlGnBu"
            - cmap="Blues"
            - cmap="BuPu"
            - cmap="Greens"
    Please refer to the notebook available on the book repo
                Miscellaneous/setting_CMAP_argument_matplotlib.ipynb
    for further details.
    - xticklabels: list
                description of x-axis label;
    - yticklabels: list
                description of y-axis label
```

Note also that if you do not know which colormap to use, you
can check the *Miscellaneous* material available on GitHub, where the
`setting_CMAP_argument_matplotlib.ipynb` file is available: tit basically shows
different colormaps that can be used to color your favourite plot.

Another question that might arise is: what happens if we increase the number of
neighbors? The next chunk produces a plot that shows the accuracy of the model
for different values of the hyperparameter n_neighbors: note that a zoom of the first
ten iteration is shown in Figure 1.4.

```
In [10]:n_neigh = list(range(1,50))
        train_scores = []
        test_scores = []
        for i in n_neigh:
            knn = KNeighborsClassifier(n_neighbors=i)
            knn.fit(X_train,y_train)
```

```
        train_score = knn.score(X_train,y_train)
        train_scores.append(train_score)
        test_score = knn.score(X_test,y_test)
        test_scores.append(test_score)
df = pd.DataFrame()
df['n_neigh']= n_neigh
df['Training Score']=train_scores
df['Test Score']=test_scores
plt.figure(figsize=(5,5))
plt.plot(df.iloc[:,0], df.iloc[:,1],
                    label ='Train Performance')
plt.plot(df.iloc[:,0], df.iloc[:,2],
                    label ='Test Performance')
plt.xlabel('Number of Neighbors', fontsize=16)
plt.ylabel('Accuracy', fontsize=16)
plt.legend()
plt.show()
```

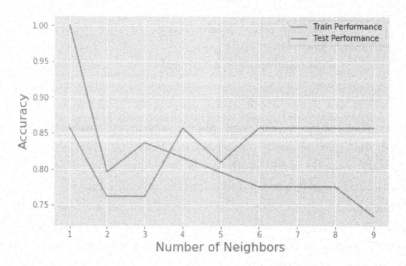

Figure 1.4: Sensitivity analysis on the accuracy for different number of Neighbors.

It seems a good choice might be n_neighbors equal to three. Obviously, as the number of Neighbors tend to zero, our model gets too complicated, and hence we poorly generalize to new data: this is called overfitting. More specifically, overfitting refers to the situation where a model is not able to well generalize to new, unseen data, and typically we have it when the model perfectly memorizes the whole training set but does not clearly separates the two classes. This might be induced by the fact we are retaining all the observed training noise, and therefore it is difficult to generalize to new data.

Underfitting, instead, refers to the situation where the model is too simple, and it is not able to extract useful information from the training set. In this case, the accuracy in both training and test set is similar, and tend to be smaller as the model gets to simpler.

Generally, in k-Nearest Neighbors, a lower number of neighbors refers to a more complex model: for regression models, as we will see in Chapter 2, we can prevent overfitting by regularizing the regression coefficients, whereas with ensemble methods we typically control it by managing the depth of the tree.

1.1.1 Tuning Hyperparameters with Cross-Validation

We saw that to train a model, we notably split the data into a training and test set. However, especially in k-Nearest Neighbors (kNN), we have to set a priori the number of neighbors, which is quite restrictive from a inferential point of view: this means that the user must know the number of clusters our data will be grouped by the training algorithm, which is actually unknown at the beginning of the data analysis.

Hence, what we can do is to train a series of kNN models, and then evaluate each model performance on the test set. But this has a major limitation: I am picking the model that best performs on the test set, which is quite restrictive because it does just depends on the data I have observed. In other words, the test set prediction is not an unbiased estimate of future performances anymore.

Instead, what we typically do is to use three folds that we split into:

- Training set, which is used for model fitting;

- Validation set, which is used for picking the (best) parameters;

- Test set for evaluating the model on unseen data.

To illustrate the real need of this strategy, let's make use of the Breast Cancer Wisconsin (Diagnostic) Data Set, available online at https://archive.ics.uci.edu/ml/datasets/Breast+Cancer+Wisconsin+(Diagnostic). The reader can find a copy of it within the book repository. Again, we read the data using the egeaML class DataIngestion.

```
In [11]: data_ = DataIngestion(df='breast_cancer_data.csv',
                    col_to_drop=None,col_target='diagnosis')
        X = data_.features()
        y = data_.target().apply(lambda x: 1 if x=='M' else 0)
```

We have not spoken about Scaling yet, but for the moment please take into account that in many applications, it is a good practice to normalize the data, so that the magnitude of each feature can be compared. Here, we scale the data, using the scikit-learn method Scale from the class preprocessing.

```
In [12]: X=scale(X)
```

We now split the data into training, validation and test set.

```
In [13]: X_train, X_test, y_train, y_test= train_test_split(X,y,
                    test_size=0.3,random_state=42)
```

```
In [14]: X_train_,X_val,y_train_,y_val = train_test_split(X_train,
                    y_train,test_size=0.3, random_state=42)
```

```
In [15]: knn = KNeighborsClassifier(n_neighbors=5).fit(
                                    X_train_,y_train_)
```

```
In [16]: print("Validation Score: {:.4f}".format(knn.score(
                                    X_val,y_val)))
        print("Test Score: {:.4f}".format(knn.score(
                                    X_test,y_test)))
```

```
Validation Score: 0.9333
Test Score: 0.9649
```

Basically we use the validation to select the parameters (in this case the n_neighbors), and then we use the test set to figure out the model to put into production. This is nice because this method is simple and fast, but it has at least one problem: it shows high variance in the test set, since it is splitted twice, and hence it depends on how you really split the data. As a corollary, another problem can be the bad use of data, which translates into the fact that if you make the validation set too small, you will have even more variance in the evaluation.

Hence, what we typically do in practice is *cross-validation*: instead of splitting the data into three folds as before, we are going to split the whole data into *n* folds of equal size. The idea of cross-validation is simple, yet powerful: we pick one fold and we fix it as the test set, whereas the other $n - 1$ folds are used to fit the model. However, instead of just doing it once, we then sequentially fix another fold as the test set, and fit the same model on the other $n - 1$ folds, hence considering the fold that was used before for testing. We repeat this procedure for all the n, non-overlapping different folds, obtaining n different scores: this is more stable because is less dependent on the split, and each data point is exactly in the test set once. Likewise, the outcome of cross-validation is made of n scores, from which for instance we can take the mean (or the median) as overall score, which is indeed a more robust estimate of how good this kind of model is on this kind of dataset. Figure 1.5 shows how cross-validation works.[1].

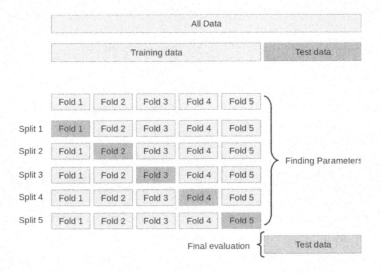

Figure 1.5: Representation of a 5-folds cross-validation. This was taken from the

If you also want to tune the parameters, you still need to have a separate test set: so a good strategy is to split the data into training and test set. You cross-validate the training set to look for the best parameters, and then you use the test set to evaluate how the choosen configuration of parameters will perform on new data. As an example, the following snippet shows for each n_neighbors the cross-validated score, and then I select the best model.

With scikit-learn we use the cross_val_score function: it basically split the data into n independent folds, and computes for each split, the accuracy on that particular split fold. Then, we pick the best score, and we pick the model parameters associated to that particular score. If we pick the best configuration, then we train the best model on the whole training set, and the test score now is indeed an unbiased estimate of well this model performs in the future.

```
In [17]: X_train,X_test, y_train, y_test = train_test_split(X,y,
                        test_size=0.3, random_state=42)
        cross_val_scores = []
        neighbors = np.arange(1,15,2)
        for i in neighbors:
            knn = KNeighborsClassifier(n_neighbors=i)
            scores = cross_val_score(knn,X_train,y_train,cv=5)
            cross_val_scores.append(np.mean(scores))

        print("Best CV Score: {:.4f}".format(np.max(
                        cross_val_scores)))
        best_nn = neighbors[np.argmax(cross_val_scores)]
        print("Best n_neighbors: {}".format(best_nn))
```

```
Best CV Score: 0.6958
Best n_neighbors: 3
```

You should have noticed a little drawback related to the cross-validation procedure shown above. Indeed, to perform cross-validation, we had to impose a priori a set of possibile values where to search for the best parameter (in our case n_neighbors). This is fine with simple models, like k-NN, but what if we had to search more than one value, possibly ranging in $\mathbb{R}$? In this scenario, we should fix all possible combinations among the parameters, which might be unmanageable for a sufficient granular grid of values. Hence, instead of randomly choosing the parameters' values, a better approach would be to use an algorithm that automatically finds the best parameters among all possible combinations of parameter values, that is the one which typically returns the combination with the highest accuracy.

To implement grid search cross validation in scikit-learn, we use the class Grid-SearchCV, which actually performs model selection and cross-validation together. To repeat its workflow, it iterates through all the parameters, and for each combination of parameters, it does cross-validation finding the best parameters. Once this is spotted, we train the best model on the whole training dataset. Note that we will use the argument stratify, which controls that the distribution of the class label is the same in both the training and test set.

```
In [18]: from sklearn.model_selection import GridSearchCV
         X_train, X_test, y_train, y_test = train_test_split(X,y,
                     stratify=y,test_size=0.3,random_state=42)
         param_grid = {'n_neighbors': np.arange(1,15,2)}
         clf = KNeighborsClassifier()
         grid = GridSearchCV(clf, param_grid= param_grid, cv=10)
         grid.fit(X_train,y_train)
         print("Best Mean CV Score: {:.4f}".format(
                                     grid.best_score_))
         print("Best Params: {}".format(grid.best_params_))
         print("Test-set Score: {:.4f}".format(grid.score(
                                     X_test,y_test)))

Best Mean CV Score: 0.8163
Best Params: {'n_neighbors': 7}
Test-set Score: 0.5714

In [19]: results = pd.DataFrame(grid.cv_results_)
         print(results.columns)
         print(results.params)

Index(['mean_fit_time', 'std_fit_time', 'mean_score_time',
       'std_score_time', 'param_n_neighbors', 'params',
       'split0_test_score', 'split1_test_score',
       'split2_test_score', 'split3_test_score',
       'split4_test_score', 'split5_test_score',
       'split6_test_score', 'split7_test_score',
       'split8_test_score', 'split9_test_score',
       'mean_test_score', 'std_test_score', 'rank_test_score'],
       dtype='object')
0      {'n_neighbors': 1}
1      {'n_neighbors': 3}
2      {'n_neighbors': 5}
3      {'n_neighbors': 7}
4      {'n_neighbors': 9}
5     {'n_neighbors': 11}
```

```
6    {'n_neighbors': 13}
Name: params, dtype: object
```

1.2   Preprocessing

To introduce the reader to such important topic, which is mainly applied to linear models, we will use the Boston House Dataset, available in the book-specific GitHub repository, where the goal is to predict the median price of the Boston's houses (MEDV).

```
In [1]: from egeaML import DataIngestion, Preprocessing
        from sklearn.neighbors import KNeighborsRegressor, KNeighborsClassifier
        from sklearn.preprocessing import StandardScaler, OneHotEncoder
        from sklearn.preprocessing import PowerTransformer
        from sklearn.model_selection import cross_val_score, GridSearchCV
        from sklearn.pipeline import make_pipeline

Using TensorFlow backend.

In [2]: reader = DataIngestion(df='boston.csv',col_target = 'MEDV')
        df = reader.load_data()
        X = reader.features()
        y = reader.target()
```

In order to get a better idea of the effect of each feature on the target variable MEDV, consider the following series of scatter plots, produced by the next snippet.

```
In [3]: plt.figure(figsize=(20, 15))
        features = list(X)
        for i, col in enumerate(features):
            plt.subplot(3, len(features)/2 , i+1)
            x = df[col]
            y = y
            plt.scatter(x, y, marker='o')
            plt.title(col)
            plt.xlabel(col)
            plt.ylabel('MEDV')
```

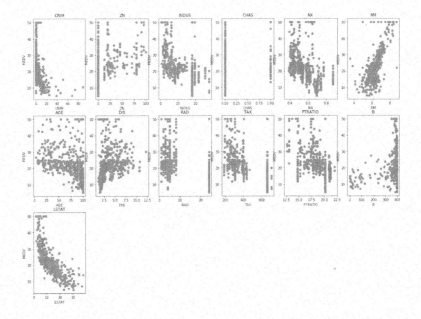

Although most of the above plots do not show a clear relationship, there are two features that clearly show some linear dependence: for instance, there is a positive linear relationship between MEDV and RM (numbers of rooms), whereas when LSTAT increases MEDV decreases. In particular, when you look at these plots it is easy to see that some of the features are continuous (e.g. LSTAT or NX), others are binary (CHAS). But more importantly, it is clear that those features are not in the same scale. Hence, a very important procedure is to scale data before fitting a ML model.

1.2.1 Scaling Data

Scaling data is very useful, especially when features have different size and magnitude. This process improves the score of the model on the test set.

```
In [4]: data_melted = pd.melt(df)
        fig = sns.boxplot(x="variable", y="value", data=data_melted)
        plt.ylabel('MEDV')
        plt.xlabel('')
        fig.set_xticklabels(fig.get_xticklabels(),rotation=30)
        plt.show()
```

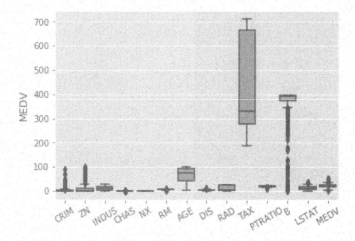

It is clear there exists an important variability among features due to the scaling effect: the magnitude on taxes is of thousands, whereas the one of age is, not surprisingly, of hundreds. Furthermore, most of them are not normally distributed, that is they are pretty skewed, and so we need to scale them before fitting a model.

Also, we do not know (a priori) which features might be considered important for our model, so scaling is a way to implicitly assign equal weight to different features that show different scale and magnitude: only after scaling we will pick the ones who explain our target the better (with the drawback of loosing some physical interpretability).

Typically, to scale data we implement the StandardScaler method in scikit-learn: this ensures that for each feature the mean is zero and the variance is one, bringing all features to the same magnitude. A different scaling is the MinMaxScaler method, scales between a minimum and a maximum value, typically zero and one but it is flexible. This is especially useful if we have to deal with some features that have fixed boundaries: for instance, if I have to squash a feature that ranges between 1 and 100, then it makes sense to use this method. If, instead, we are dealing with data that comes from an extrem-value distribution, probably this method does not make sense at all. Another one is the RobustScaler, which works similarly to the Standard one but uses the median and the quantiles, instead of the mean and variance: this is definitely useful when one has (or suspect to have) outliers, since the median is known to be robust with respect to them. Finally, one can use the Normalizer method, which is especially used with count data: the granularity here is each single row, and normalize each feature vector so that it has a $\mathcal{L}_2$-norm equal to one. Note that it allows also for other norms, such as the $\mathcal{L}_1$-norm, which basically translates into a normalization by the sum of absolute values (and its length should be equal to one).

Remark. Sparse dataset are the ones with many zeros: those are very common in genetics, text analysis and even in fraud detection. A practical problem one might encounter is that typically we don't want to store (all) the zeros but only the ones: this is not easy, since storing say 100,000 zeros for each single row will blow up the RAM of your local machine. In this scenario, it does not make any sense to use, say, the StandardScaler, because we would subtract a non-zero mean from a zero-value record, which might affect negatively the scaling, and affecting the usage of RAM.

Coming back to the Boston Dataset, we now try to apply the StandardScaler to the set of features, and then compare the performances between the unscaled and the scaled dataset..

```
In [5]: X_train, X_test, y_train, y_test= train_test_split(X,y
                       , test_size=0.3,random_state=42)
```

Our simpler example on the Boston Dataset will be based on the StandardScaler method and on a Regression Task using the KNeighborsRegressor method, which is basically a more sophisticated model when the target is continuous, as in this case (i.e. MEDV). Before scaling the data, let us see how the model performs on unscaled data.

```
In [6]: scores_unscaled = cross_val_score(KNeighborsRegressor(),
                       X_train, y_train,cv=5)
        scores_unscaled
```

```
Out[6]: array([0.63515605, 0.17772906, 0.34902784, 0.43737922, 0.37189903])
```

Since we are cross-validating the model, we obtain as many scores as the number of splits (in this case, five). Hence, a good summary measure of model performance is to take the average of the scores, as follows:

```
In [7]: np.mean(scores_unscaled), np.std(scores_unscaled)
```

```
Out[7]: (0.3942382409253963, 0.14786600926386584)
```

To scale the data, we instanciate the Python class StandardScaler, and we call the fit method on the scaler object : this practically means computing the mean and standard deviation on the training data, whereas the transform on the train data basically subtract the mean and divide by the standard deviation each single data point in the training set.

```
In [8]: scaler = StandardScaler()
        scaler.fit(X_train)
        X_train_scaled = scaler.transform(X_train)
        X_test_scaled = scaler.transform(X_test)

In [9]: scores_scaled = cross_val_score(KNeighborsRegressor(),
                X_train_scaled, y_train,cv=5)
        np.mean(scores_scaled), np.std(scores_scaled)

Out[9]: (0.7009222608410279, 0.029897124253597467)
```

We see that the performance increases significatively by scaling the data. But be careful: different scaling methods lead to different results, which requires either proper Exploratory Data Analysis (EDA) or good attention from the researcher to understand the best method to apply. Last, but not least, one should note that when we run the scikit-learn cross_val_score method, we have used the entire scaled training dataset: this means that for each different split done in cross-validation, its corresponding test fold was already used to find the proper scaling, which therefore violates the independence assumption that we require from the training and the test set to have unbiased estimates. In other words, we are *leaking* information from the test set to find the optimal scaling! Furthermore, when we go into production, new, unseen data comes into the model, but that set is not going to be used to scale the training dataset, and therefore could have different scaling and values. To overcome to this problem, we fit the scaling on only the training dataset, and evaluate the model performances on the validation set using cross-validation. In order to avoid this kind of problems, we use the Pipeline class, which allows to perform the splitting phase within the cross-validation by chaining these two steps.

```
In [10]: pipeline = make_pipeline(StandardScaler(),
                                    KNeighborsRegressor())
         scores_pipe = cross_val_score(pipeline, X_train,
                                    y_train,cv=5)
         np.mean(scores_pipe), np.std(scores_pipe)

Out[10]: (0.6944726314773543, 0.028669555232832964)
```

Note that the pipeline object sequentially applies a list of transforms and a final estimator, which only requires to implement the fit method. For a better introduction of this class, please visit the online documentation at https://scikit-learn.org/stable/modules/generated/sklearn.pipeline.Pipeline.html. We can also perform Grid Search within pipelines as follows:

```
In [11]:  par_grid = {'kneighborsregressor__n_neighbors': range(1,10)}
          grid = GridSearchCV(pipeline, par_grid=param_grid,cv=5)
          grid.fit(X_train, y_train)
          print("Number of Neighbors Best Parameter: ",
          grid.best_params_['kneighborsregressor__n_neighbors'])
          print("Score on Test set: {:.4f}".format(grid.score(
                                X_test,y_test)))

Number of Neighbors Best Parameter:   2
Score on Test set: 0.7887
```

1.2.2 Forcing Data to be Gaussian: an Introduction to Power Transformations

In the next plot we have the feature distribution after scaling: although we have standardized the features, we still see they show different distributions: for instance, the feature B is really skewed, whereas the PTRATIO looks completely different.

```
In [12]:  scaler = StandardScaler()
          scaler.fit(X)
          X_scaled = scaler.transform(X)
          plt.boxplot(X_scaled)
          plt.xticks(np.arange(1,X.shape[1]+1), list(X), rotation=30)
          plt.ylabel('MEDV')
          plt.show()
```

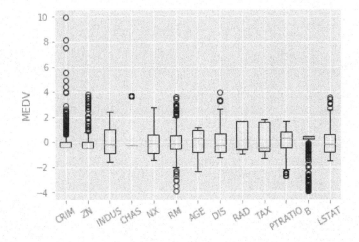

A way to make this data more Gaussian (or at least more behaved) is to use Power Transformations such as the well-known Box-Cox Transform, introduced by Box and Cox (1964), defined as follows:

$$BC_\lambda(x) = \begin{cases} \frac{x^\lambda - 1}{\lambda} & \text{if} \quad \lambda \neq 0 \\ \log(x) & \text{if} \quad \lambda = 0 \end{cases}$$

The idea is to raise your data x to some power, λ. Note, however, that this is only applicable to non-negative data points, so be careful when trying to applying this transformation: in principle, a good practice is to take the absolute value of your data, but this decision is up to the scientist. Alternatively, one can use the Yeo and Johnson (1997) power transformation, which accomodates for both positive and negative values.

```
In [13]: pt = PowerTransformer(method='yeo-johnson')
         data_gauss = pt.fit_transform(X_scaled)

In [14]: print("------ Before Power Transformation ------")
         classification_plots.plot_hist(X_scaled,features,'MEDV')
```

```
------ Before Power Transformation ------
```

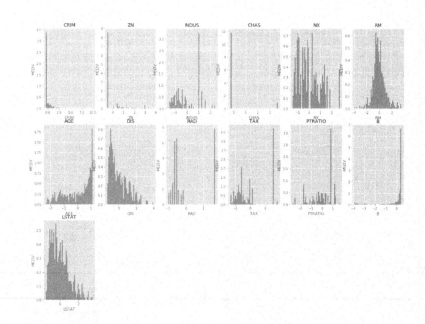

```
In [15]: print("------ After Power Transformation ------")
         classification_plots.plot_hist(data_gauss,features,'MEDV')
```

`------ After Power Transformation ------`

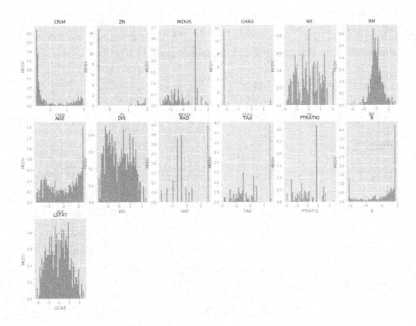

1.2.3   Dealing with Categorical Variables

A categorical variable describes a particular class of features that is characterized by assuming a finite number of values. We introduce how to deal with categorical variables in Python by showing two different methods: one using the Pandas API and another one using scikit-learn. For the sake of illustration, we will use a toy dataset containing the data of a series of Italian restaurants.

```
In [16]: reader = DataIngestion(df='restaurant.csv',col_target = 'tip')
         data = reader.load_data()
```

```
In [17]: data.head()
```

```
Out[17]:    total_bill  tip     city    sex smoker  day    time size
        0        16.99  Yes    Milan Female    Yes  Sat   Lunch    2
        1        10.34   No     Rome   Male     No  Sun  Dinner    3
        2        21.01   No  Bergamo   Male     No  Mon  Dinner    3
        3        23.68   No   Naples   Male     No  Sun  Dinner    2
        4        24.59  Yes    Milan Female     No  Fri  Dinner    4
```

We see that, apart from the target variable tip, there are five categorical variables in this toy dataset: city, sex, smoker, day and time. However, we expect our features to be real numbers, so we need to convert them somehow before training our model. One possible way is to apply *Ordinal Encoding*, which actually assigns a real number to each distinct value in the categorical variable.

```
In [18]: categorical_variables = ['city','sex','smoker','day','time']
```

```
In [19]: data['day_ord']= data['day'].astype("category").cat.codes
```

```
In [20]: data.head()
```

```
Out[20]:    total_bill  tip     city     sex smoker  day    time  size  day_ord
         0        16.99  Yes    Milan  Female    Yes  Sat   Lunch     2        2
         1        10.34   No     Rome    Male     No  Sun  Dinner     3        3
         2        21.01   No  Bergamo    Male     No  Mon  Dinner     3        1
         3        23.68   No   Naples    Male     No  Sun  Dinner     2        3
         4        24.59  Yes    Milan  Female     No  Fri  Dinner     4        0
```

This procedure is fine but has some drawbacks: for instance, it creates and imposes an ordering on the values. For the day variable, that is fine, but there might be, say, a column that indicates the city where the restaurant is, and there there is no meaning on imposing an (arbitrary) order. A solution for this is to use the *Dummy Encoding*, using the Pandas function get_dummies, also called OneHotEncoding in the scikit-learn framework. In particular, what we are doing is adding a new feature (actually a new column in the dataframe) for each possible value of the categorical variable. This is easily implemented in Pandas, as follows:

```
In [21]: data_dummized = pd.get_dummies(data,prefix_sep='_',
                            prefix=categorical_variables,
                            columns=categorical_variables,
                            drop_first=False)
```

Note that this function categorizes variables that are either objects or categorical, but we can control which variable is going to be encoded by using the columns attribute inside the function call. Note also that we have used all the available data to perform the dummization: there is no problem on doing that, especially if we want to set up a production system, where new data comes fresh into the model, but we need to categorize *a priori* which classes are admissible. For instance, we have not observed the city of Trento in the training set, but in production it might happen to observe it. Obviously, we cannot learn anything from it but if there is a valid motivation to

include it, we might encode it in the training set even though we have not observed
it. To do that, we might use the Categorical method from Pandas:

```
In [22]: cat=['Milan', 'Rome', 'Bergamo',
              'Naples', 'Como', 'Trieste',
              'Brescia', 'Turin', 'Florence', 'Trento']
         data['city']=pd.Categorical(data['city'],categories=cat)
         pd.get_dummies(data, columns=['city']).head()
```

Out[22]:

	total_bill	tip	sex	smoker	day	time	size	day_ord	city_Milan	\
0	16.99	Yes	Female	Yes	Sat	Lunch	2	2	1	
1	10.34	No	Male	No	Sun	Dinner	3	3	0	
2	21.01	No	Male	No	Mon	Dinner	3	1	0	
3	23.68	No	Male	No	Sun	Dinner	2	3	0	
4	24.59	Yes	Female	No	Fri	Dinner	4	0	1	

	city_Rome	city_Bergamo	city_Naples	city_Como	city_Trieste	\
0	0	0	0	0	0	
1	1	0	0	0	0	
2	0	1	0	0	0	
3	0	0	1	0	0	
4	0	0	0	0	0	

	city_Brescia	city_Turin	city_Florence	city_Trento
0	0	0	0	0
1	0	0	0	0
2	0	0	0	0
3	0	0	0	0
4	0	0	0	0

In scikit-learn, the Dummy Encoding is applied via the OneHotEncoding class: it as-
sumes that all the columns we give to the method are categorical, which is not optimal in many cases, since we typically have both categorical and continuous features
in the dataset. The following snippet produces the output obtained from the application of that method to the entire data:

```
In [23]: ohe = OneHotEncoder().fit(data)
         ohe.transform(data).toarray()
```

```
Out[23]: array([[0., 0., 0., ..., 0., 0., 0.],
                [0., 0., 0., ..., 0., 0., 0.],
                [0., 0., 0., ..., 0., 0., 0.],
                ...,
                [0., 0., 1., ..., 0., 1., 0.],
```

```
[0., 0., 0., ..., 0., 0., 1.],
[0., 0., 0., ..., 0., 0., 0.]])
```

In the scikit-learn version 0.20.0 a new way of transforming categorical variables was introduced: this is called Column Transformer, which works similarly to the Pipeline class. In particular, not only does it give us the possibility to put together several transformations into a single step, but it also allows one to select which columns to transform using a certain transformer.

```
In [24]: from sklearn.compose import make_column_transformer
```

```
In [25]: categ = data.dtypes == object
         preprocess = make_column_transformer(
                          (StandardScaler(), ~categ),
                          (OneHotEncoder(),categ))
         model = make_pipeline(preprocess, KNeighborsClassifier() )
```

The previous step basically works as follows:

1. We define which variables are categoricals;

2. We tell the machine that whichever column is not categorical, then a Standard-Scaler transformation is applied; else, a OneHotEncoder is used;

3. This is put together into a pipeline that fits a Classifier.

Note that the OneHotEncoder can introduce collinearity, and it can be an issue for non-penalized linear models, which are going to be discussed in Chapter 2.

1.2.4   Handling with Missing Values

Another, very common preprocessing step that any scientist perform before fitting the model is the so called *Imputation* of the missing values. This is very common, in practice, for many reasons, and we are not going to discuss here the motivation of why this happens. However, take into account that typically one has two strategies:

1. Remove the example that shows one (or more) missing values;

2. Impute the missing value with a reasonable summary statistics

We now show the second option, using the method spotting_null_values from the book-specific Preprocessing Class. To better undertand what this class does, we use syntetich data, so that the user can actually visualize the usage of this function:

```
In [26]: data_ = pd.DataFrame({'col1':[np.nan,2,4,8,10],
                               'col2':[23,26,28,32,40],
                               'col3':[11000, 9500, np.nan,
                                       np.nan, 14760]},
                              columns = ['col1','col2','col3'])

In [27]: data_

Out[27]:     col1  col2      col3
         0   NaN   23    11000.0
         1   2.0   26     9500.0
         2   4.0   28        NaN
         3   8.0   32        NaN
         4  10.0   40    14760.0
```

The function performs two main operations: firstly, it looks for the type of the column we are focusing on: if it is of type object, then it computes the mode of that column; it is continuous, then it computes the median, which is a robust statistics to outliers. Then, for each row, it looks for any possible missing value: if one is spotted, then its value is inputed, taking into account the type of the column and the value computed in the first step. We use the book-specific function spotting_null_values to do that.

```
In [28]: Preprocessing(list(data_),data_).spotting_null_values()

Out[30]:     col1  col2      col3
         0   6.0   23    11000.0
         1   2.0   26     9500.0
         2   4.0   28    11000.0
         3   8.0   32    11000.0
         4  10.0   40    14760.0
```

Note that this operation should be done before applying any scaling. A different case, which is worth to be mentioned here, is the imputation of categorical variables: in many applications, it is better to leave the empty category within the dummization phase, which is reasonable especially when you have to deal with particular categories. An example could be the type of transaction from a credit card: if that is not available, it does not make any sense to impute its value with the mode, because we would put some biased information in the data, not corresponding to the reality.

Meanwhile this book was written, a new version of scikit-learn went out (version 0.21.0), where the interest reader can find a new, dynamic, and powerful imputing method, called IterativeImputer, from the Impute class, which is a clever strategy for imputing missing values by modeling each feature with missing values as a function of other features using a supervised learning model. We basically pick each column, and use it as a target, while using the other $k-1$ features as input of the choosen supervised model (e.g. Random Forest or Linear Regressor), and then one uses that model to predict on the missing values.

1.3   Methods for Dealing with Imbalanced Data

So far we have focused on a few important characteristics that, globally, distinguish a dataset, namely how to deal with categorical variables (or missing values), and to scale the data. The dataset preprocessing is probably the most important step in building a ML model, since its outcome is going to be strictly dependent on that step. However, real datasets deal with many others possible features that we have not discussed yet: among many, it is worth to mention the issue of imbalanced datasets. Imbalanced datasets often arise in classification problems where the classes are not equally distributed among the examples. Unfortunately, this is quite a common problem in Machine Learning and Computer Vision, since we might not have a sufficient number of training examples that allows to correctly predict the minority class. This issue affects different areas, including cancer diagnosis using f-MRI, cyber security, and financial crime. As an example, insurance companies are investing resources in constructing ML pipelines to detect fraudolent behaviours in reported claims. Luckily, most of them are not fraudolent, and just a few of belong instead to the positive class (i.e. the fraudolent one). As a consequence, if we try to fit a classifier on such an imbalanced dataset, it is likely to get a biased model, since the classifier always predicts the most common training class, regarding the examples values, and therefore getting a very high accuracy. As an example, let us try to fit a simple knn classifier on the imbalanced Kaggle Credit Card Fraud Detection dataset available at the following link: https://www.kaggle.com/mlg-ulb/creditcardfraud. This dataset contains European credit card transactions, and 492 out of 284,807 transactions were labelled as frauds.

```
In [29]:   from egeaML import DataIngestion
           from sklearn.utils import resample
           from imblearn.over_sampling import SMOTE
```

Using TensorFlow backend.

```
In [30]: di = DataIngestion(df='creditcard.csv', col_to_drop=None,
                            col_target='Class')
         df = di.load_data()
         title = ' Imbalanced Credit Card Fraud Dataset'
         di.plot_counts('Class', 'title')
```

Out[30]: <matplotlib.axes._subplots.AxesSubplot at 0x1a346f6400>

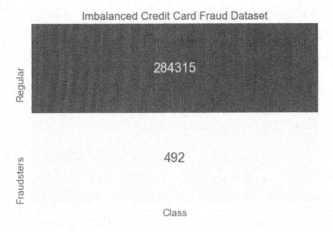

```
In [31]: X = di.features()
         y = di.target()
```

```
In [32]: X_train, X_test, y_train, y_test = di.split_train_test(
             test_size=0.3, random_seed=42)
```

We now fit a simple knn model, and look at its performances on this imbalanced dataset.

```
In [33]: knn = KNeighborsClassifier(n_neighbors=1)
         knn.fit(X_train,y_train)
         y_pred = knn.predict(X_test)
         score = knn.score(X_test,y_test)
         print("accuracy: {:.4f}".format(score))
```

accuracy: 0.9984

Not surprisingly, we get an illusory, almost perfect accuracy, since the 395 frauds account for only the 0.1785% of all training transactions. Therefore, when dealing with imbalanced datasets in a classification framework, accuracy is not anymore a good metric. Therefore, we have (at least) three different possibilities to tackle this problem:

1. Changing the algorithm: this might be a simple choice, but sometimes it increases the performances on the negative class. A very popular choice is nowadays the family of ensemble methods, which are discussed in Chapter 3;

2. Changing the evaluation metric: instead of using accuracy, we might use precision or recall (to investigate these concepts, please refer to Chapter 2 in the section on Classification);

3. Resorting to Resampling Techniques: this strategy has been widely used in the computer vision community to resample images when the datasets were too small to train a image recognizer. Nowadays, this is widely used in ML when one has to face a shortage of data in a given class.

In this Section, we will focus on resampling techniques that allow to either oversample the minority class or undersample the majority class.

1.3.1   Random Oversampling of the Majority Class

This situation refers to adding more examples to the minority class: although this simple, yet powerful, strategy allows one to get balanced classes, the major drawback of this technique is that it simply add duplicates of the previous examples, increasing the possibility of overfitting. To do so, we use the scikit-learn function resample. Note that since we aim to upsample the minority class, we would like the minority to have the same lenght of the majority class by setting n_samples equal to len(\textsf{majority_class}).

```
In [34]: train, test = train_test_split(df,
                                         test_size=0.3,
                                         random_state=42)

In [35]: major_class = train[train.Class==0]
         minority_class = train[train.Class==1]
         upsampled_class = resample(minority_class,
                                    replace=True,
```

```
                                   n_samples=len(major_class),
                                   random_state=27)
        upsampled_data = pd.concat([major_class, upsampled_class])

In [36]: plt.figure(figsize=(8, 5))
         t='Balanced Classes after upsampling.'
         upsampled_data.Class.value_counts().plot(kind='bar', title=t)

Out[36]: <matplotlib.axes._subplots.AxesSubplot at 0x1153d0e80>
```

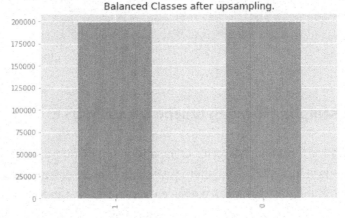

1.3.2 Random Undersampling of the Majority Class

This situation refers to removing examples from the majority class. Note that the major drawback of this technique is that removing units from the majority class might cause a significant loss of information in the training set, which translates into possible underfitting.

```
In [37]: down_class = resample(major_class,
                               replace=False,
                               n_samples=len(minority_class),
                               random_state=27)

         downsampled_data = pd.concat([down_class, minority_class])

In [38]: plt.figure(figsize=(8, 5))
         t='Balanced Classes after upsampling.'
         downsampled_data.Class.value_counts().plot(kind='bar', title=t)

Out[38]: <matplotlib.axes._subplots.AxesSubplot at 0x1a35e92b70>
```

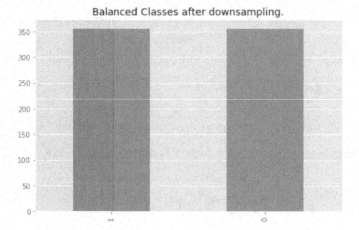

1.3.3   Oversampling using Synthetic Data: SMOTE

SMOTE stands for Synthetic Minority Oversampling TEchnique, and it was proposed by Chawla et al. (2002) as an alternative to random oversampling. How does it works? Well, it merges two ideas we have deepen so far: random sampling and k-nearest neighbours. Indeed, SMOTE allows to create new data from the minority class (they are not copy of the observed one, as in random resampling), and automatically computes the k-nns for those points. The synthetic points are added between the chosen point and its neighbors. Note that the imblearn API, which is part of the scikit-learn project, is used to apply the SMOTE in the following snippet.

```
In [39]: smote = SMOTE(sampling_strategy='minority')
         X_smote, y_smote = smote.fit_sample(X_train, y_train)
         X_smote = pd.DataFrame(X_smote, columns=X_train.columns )
         y_smote = pd.DataFrame(y_smote, columns=['Class'])


In [40]: smote_data = pd.concat([X_smote,y_smote],axis=1)
         plt.figure(figsize=(8, 5))
         title='Balanced Classes using SMOTE'
         smote_data.Class.value_counts().plot(kind='bar', title=title)


Out[40]: <matplotlib.axes._subplots.AxesSubplot at 0x1a36e25080>
```

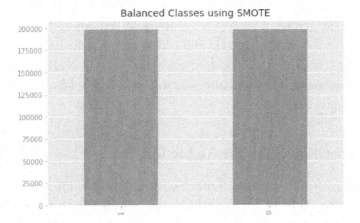

Note that when the parameter sampling_strategy is equal to minority, this forces the algorithm to resample only the minority class with a corresponding ratio of 1:1.

1.4 Reducing Dimensionality: Principal Component Analysis

In the modern era of machine learning, people involved in data science have to deal with a large number of variables. For example, in computer vision problems, we have to deal with images classification, which machine representation is on term of pixels. In order to make quantitative analysis, those pixels are described as quantitative (binary) variables. But a natural question is: how many pixels does an image have? If we pick a modern 4K image, its resolution is 3840 x 2160 pixels, and so to process such image, we need to take into account 24, 883, 200 variables (just multiply the number of pixels by the three color channels, i.e. blue, red and green).

This is a huge amount of features, and dealing with all of them might be extremely painful for many machine learning algorithms. Indeed, high dimensionality increases the computational complexity, as well as it increases the risk of overfitting and the chances of having sparsity. Hence, it is good practice to reduce the dimensionality of the problem by *projecting the data* into a space with less dimension, which allows to control these effects.

There exists a large number of dimensionality reduction techniques known in literature, but we will focus on the Principal Component Analysis.

Principal component analysis is one of the oldest and best known methods for reducing dimensionality in multivariate problems. It basically aims at finding a few principal components that contain as much information on the dependent variable as the

one contained in the original set of predictors: this original set of variables is transformed into a smaller set of linear combinations, called principal components (PC).
These new variables are uncorrelated and ordered so that the first PC accounts for
the largest proportion of the variation present in the original set of features. Note that
in regression problems, it is essentially used to prevent (or at least reduce) collinearity among independent variables.

1.4.1   PCA as dimensionality reduction

PCA basically rotates the dataset so that the rotated features are statistically uncorrelated. This rotation is often followed by selecting the principal components, according to how important they are for explaining the data. The algorithm works as
follows: we look for the vector (or direction) in the data that contains most of the
information, that is the direction along which the features are most correlated with
each other. Then, the algorithm finds the direction that contains the most information while being orthogonal (at a right angle) to the first direction, and so on. In
two dimensions, there is only one possible orientation, that is at a right angle, but in
higher-dimensional spaces there would be (infinitely) many orthogonal directions.
Note that the length of each vector is an indication of how important that axis is in
describing the distribution of the data, that is it is a measure of the variance of the
data when projected onto the axis. The projection of each data point onto the principal axes are indeed the principal components of the data.
As an illustrative example, let's consider the following toy dataset, which is shown
in Figure 1.6:

```
In [41]: rng = np.random.RandomState(1)
         X = np.dot(rng.rand(2, 2), rng.randn(2, 200)).T
         plt.scatter(X[:, 0], X[:, 1], alpha=0.2)
         plt.axis('equal')
```

Using PCA for dimensionality reduction means using only a few components, resulting in a lower-dimensional representation of the original dataset that preserves
the maximal data variance. This is easily achieved in scikit-learn, using the methods
fit_transform from the class PCA: in this example, the original data are reduced to a
single dimension.

```
In [42]: pca = PCA(n_components=1)
         X_pca = pca.fit_transform(X)
```

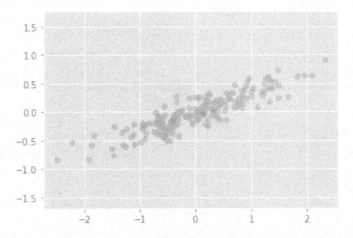

Figure 1.6: Principal Component Analysis: Scatter Plot of the Original Data

```
print("original shape:    ", X.shape)
print("transformed shape:", X_pca.shape)
```

```
original shape:     (200, 2)
transformed shape: (200, 1)
```

The following plot, shown in Figure 1.7, shows the effect of this dimensionality reduction on the original data:

```
In [43]: X_new = pca.inverse_transform(X_pca)
         plt.scatter(X[:, 0], X[:, 1], alpha=0.2)
         plt.scatter(X_new[:, 0], X_new[:, 1], alpha=0.8)
         plt.axis('equal');
```

The orange dots are the original data, while the blue ones are the projected version. This makes clear what a PCA dimensionality reduction means: the information along the least important principal axis or axes is removed, leaving only the component(s) of the data with the highest variance. Notably, the fraction of variance that is cut out (proportional to the spread of points about the line formed in this figure) is roughly a measure of how much information is discarded in this reduction of dimensionality.

```
In [44]: print(pca.explained_variance_)
```

```
[ 0.7625315]
```

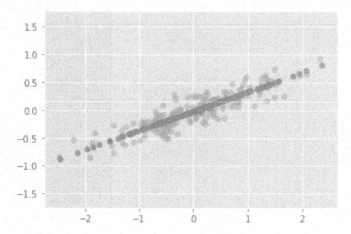

Figure 1.7: Transformation and Dimensionality reduction on a simple 2-dim feature space.

When dealing with real-data, you should remember to scale the data before applying PCA, otherwise the magnitude of the larger features will dominate the first component with respect to other components. Let's see, in practice, what this means on the breast cancer data. Note that the attribute fit_transform transforms the data onto the first $n = 2$ principal components. The result is shown in Figure 1.8.

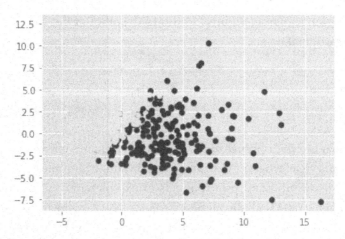

Figure 1.8: Transformation of the two Principal Components after Scaling.

```
In [45]: from sklearn.pipeline import make_pipeline
         from sklearn.datasets import load_breast_cancer
         df = load_breast_cancer()
```

```
        pca = make_pipeline(StandardScaler(),PCA(n_components=2))
        X_pca = pca.fit_transform(df.data)
        plt.scatter(X_pca[:,0], X_pca[:,1], c=df.target)
```

Out[45]: <matplotlib.collections.PathCollection at 0x1a1ad75e48>

In [46]: components = pca.named_steps['pca'].components_
        plt.imshow(components.T)
        plt.yticks(range(len(df.feature_names)), df.feature_names)
        plt.colorbar()
        plt.show()

As shown in Figure 1.9, all features now (with scaling) contribute to the first principal component. Note that if scaling is not performed, then some features will have larger magnitude, and the ones with larger magnitude will contribute to the first component. From Figure 1.9 we can also see that in the first component, all features have the same sign. That means that there is a general correlation between all features. As one measurement is high, the others are likely to be high as well. The second component has mixed signs, and both of the components involve all of the 30 features.

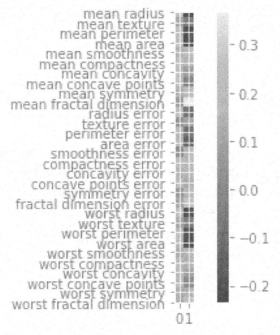

Figure 1.9: Impact of each feature on the first two Principal Components.

1.4.2   Feature extraction

We introduced PCA as an algorithm that transforms the original data by rotating them and then dropping the components with lower variance retention. Another application of PCA is feature extraction. The idea behind feature extraction is that it is possible to find a (linear) representation of your data that better describes the data. In other words, the objective is to try to find some numbers, that is the new feature values after the PCA rotation, so that we can express the test points as a weighted sum of the principal components.

We will give a very simple application of feature extraction on images using PCA, by working with face images from the Labeled Faces in the Wild dataset. This dataset contains face images of celebrities downloaded from the Internet, and it includes faces of politicians, singers, actors, and athletes from the early 2000s. There are 3,023 images, each 62×47 pixels large, belonging to 62 different people.

Hence, we have 2914 features, and we would like to use PCA to reduce the dimensionality of the problem.

```
In [47]: from sklearn.datasets import fetch_lfw_people
         faces = fetch_lfw_people(min_faces_per_person=20)
         print("Image Shape: {}".format(faces.images.shape))
         print("Number of Features: {}".format(faces.data.shape[1]))
         print("Number of classes: {}".format(len(faces.target_names)))
         X = faces.data
         y=faces.target
```

```
Image Shape: (3023, 62, 47)
Number of Features: 2914
Number of classes: 62
```

A common task in face recognition is to ask if a previously unseen face belongs to a known person from a database. This has applications in photo collections, social media, and security applications. One way to solve this problem would be to build a classifier where each person is a separate class. However, there are usually many different people in face databases, and very few images of the same person (i.e. very few training examples per class). That makes it hard to train most classifiers. A simple solution is to use a 1-nearest neighbor classifier that looks for the most similar face image to the face you are classifying.

```
In [48]: X_train, X_test, y_train, y_test = train_test_split(X, y,
                       stratify=y,random_state=0)
```

```
print(X_train.shape)
knn = KNeighborsClassifier(n_neighbors=1)
knn.fit(X_train, y_train)
print("Test set score of 1-nn: {:.2f}".format(knn.score(
                  X_test, y_test)))
```

```
(2267, 2914)
Test set score of 1-nn: 0.33
```

We obtain an accuracy of 33%, which is not actually that bad for a 62-class classification problem. Note that random guessing would give us approximately 1.5% accuracy, but that is also not great. We correctly identify a person every third time. We firstly note that here we have more features than samples, which might be a problem with many standard algorithms. Likewise, PCA can only handle as many components as the minimum between features and samples.

```
In [49]: pca = PCA(n_components=100, whiten=True,
                            random_state=0).fit(X_train)
        X_train_pca = pca.transform(X_train)
        X_test_pca = pca.transform(X_test)
        print("X_train_pca.shape: {}".format(X_train_pca.shape))
        knn = KNeighborsClassifier(n_neighbors=1)
        knn.fit(X_train_pca, y_train)
        print("Test set score of 1-nn: {:.2f}".
        format(knn.score(X_test_pca, y_test)))
```

```
X_train_pca.shape: (2267, 100)
Test set score of 1-nn: 0.46
```

We have improved accuracy by approximately 40% by reducing the dimensionality of the problem, even by using a simple algorithm as 1-nn!

1.4.3   Nonlinear Manifold Algorithm: t-SNE

PCA is a method of constructing a particular linear transformation which results in new coordinates of the samples with very well defined properties (such as orthogonality between the different components). In other words, PCA works well only when data is basically linearly separable. Typically, when we do not have such kind of data, we use manifold learning algorithm, such as t-SNE to compute a new representation of the (training) data, without actually transforming them as in PCA. The key idea is to find a 2-dim representation of the data that preserves the distances between points as best as possible.

t-SNE is an algorithm proposed by van der Maaten and Hinton in 2008, designed with a different goal in mind, that is the ability to group *similar* data points even in a context of lack of linearity. However, while t-SNE is very good at tackling the particular goal of clustering similar samples, it has a major disadvantage compared to PCA: it gives you a low-dimensional representation of your data, but it does not give you a transformation. In other words, you cannot interpret the dimensions in a similar way you interpret the components in a PCA. It might be, therefore, useful to explore multidimensional data, but that might not be useful to interpret tasks that requires a physical interpretation of the ML models (like the example we saw when applying the PCA to Logistic regression). t-SNE are extremely used in genetics, especially in next generation sequencing,ro evaluate single-cell transcriptomic data.

```
In [40]: from sklearn.datasets import load_digits
         digits = load_digits()
         pca = PCA(n_components=2)
         pca.fit(digits.data)
         digits_pca = pca.transform(digits.data)
         colors = ["#476A2A", "#7851B8", "#BD3430", "#4A2D4E",
                   "#875525", "#A83683", "#4E655E", "#853541",
                   "#3A3120", "#535D8E"]
         plt.figure(figsize=(10, 10))
         plt.xlim(digits_pca[:, 0].min(), digits_pca[:, 0].max())
         plt.ylim(digits_pca[:, 1].min(), digits_pca[:, 1].max())
         for i in range(len(digits.data)):
                 plt.text(digits_pca[i, 0], digits_pca[i, 1],
                         str(digits.target[i]),
                         color = colors[digits.target[i]],
                         fontdict={'weight': 'bold', 'size': 9})
         plt.xlabel("First principal component")
         plt.ylabel("Second principal component")


Out[40]: Text(0,0.5,'Second principal component')
```

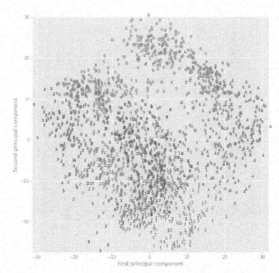

The classes zero, six, and four are relatively well separated using the first two principal components, though they still overlap. Most of the other digits overlap significantly. Let's apply t-SNE to the same dataset, and compare the results. As t-SNE does not support transforming new data, the TSNE class has no transform method. Instead, we can call the fit_transform attribute, which will build the model and immediately return the transformed data.

```
In [41]: from sklearn.manifold import TSNE
         tsne = TSNE(random_state=42, perplexity=30)
         digits_tsne = tsne.fit_transform(digits.data)

In [42]: plt.figure(figsize=(10, 10))
         plt.xlim(digits_tsne[:, 0].min(), digits_tsne[:, 0].max() + 1)
         plt.ylim(digits_tsne[:, 1].min(), digits_tsne[:, 1].max() + 1)
         for i in range(len(digits.data)):
                 plt.text(digits_tsne[i, 0], digits_tsne[i, 1],
                         str(digits.target[i]),
                         color = colors[digits.target[i]],
                         fontdict={'weight': 'bold', 'size': 9})
         plt.xlabel("t-SNE feature 0")
         plt.xlabel("t-SNE feature 1")

Out[42]: Text(0.5,0,'t-SNE feature 1')
```

The result obtained with t-SNE is quite remarkable. All the classes are quite clearly separated. The ones and nines are somewhat split up, but most of the classes form

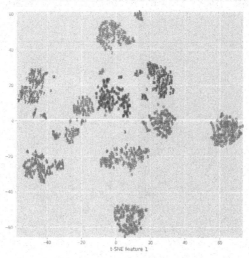

Figure 1.10: Application of t-SNE on the digits dataset.

a single dense group. Keep in mind that this method has no knowledge of the class labels: it is completely unsupervised. Still, it can find a representation of the data in two dimensions that clearly separates the classes, solely based on how close points are in the original space.

Chapter 2

Linear Models for Machine Learning

One of the most simplest supervised machine learning techniques is the family of regression models. A regression model is used to predict a continuous response variable based on a set of features. In particular, here we will focus on linear models, which actually translates into the assumption that the response variable can be expressed as a linear combination of the given features. We will then move to shrinkage methods in regression analysis, and discuss some properties and relationship of the proposed models. In the last part of this Chapter, Logistic Regression and SVM are discussed.

```
In [1]: from egeaML import DataIngestion, plots
        from sklearn.linear_model import LinearRegression, Ridge,
                            Lasso, ElasticNet
        from sklearn.model_selection import cross_val_score,
                            GridSearchCV, train_test_split
        from sklearn.metrics import mean_squared_error
```

To illustrate the methods in this section, we make use of the Boston House data, which is available within the specific-book library egeaML. We wish to predict the median value of the house based of some features. Typically, the features are separated from the target variable - i.e. the median value - and we split the dataset into training set, i.e. the dataset we are going to use to train the model, and test set.

```
In [2]: di = DataIngestion(df='boston.csv',col_to_drop=None,
                            col_target='MEDV')
```

```
X = di.features()
y = di.target()
X_train, X_test, y_train, y_test= train_test_split(X,y,
                    test_size=0.3,random_state=42)
```

The interest reader can refer to the well-written, more theoretical book by Friedman et al. (2008), which is considered the main reference for anyone who aims to deepen her knowledge on the theory behind the main machine learning methods. I strongly encourage this book for anyone who wants to get a better understanding of penalized methods, proposed in this Chapter.

2.1   Linear Regression

The most simplest model we might employ for the analysis of the Boston data is the Ordinary Least Square regression model (OLS). Its objective is to find the vector of parameters, denoted by β, so that it minimizes the residuals' sum of squares, which is equivalent to say that the prediction $\hat{y}$ should, in the training set, be much closer as possible to the true y,

$$\min_{\beta \in \mathbb{R}^p} \sum_{i=1}^{p} ||\beta^T x_i - y_i||^2$$

Be careful: features should not be linearly dependent (i.e. absence of collinearity) and full rank assumption in order the $\hat{\beta}$ to be unique.

To fit a linear regression model, scikit-learn requires a very simple recipe, which consists of two simple commands, shown below:

```
In [3]: reg = LinearRegression()
        fit = reg.fit(X_train,y_train)
        print('Regression R2 Score: {:.4f}'.format(reg.score(
                            X_test,y_test)))
```

```
Regression R2 Score: 0.7112
```

We have trained a linear model but now we would like to see the model performance on unseen data. Hence, we fit the model on the test data, and evaluate its performance using the RMSE as score metric.

Note that the R^2 is a normalized version of the MSE, but we typically use the MSE as the reporting metric since it is the loss-function we are trying to minimize. However, R^2 is useful since it does not depend on the scale of the data, and it is easily interpretable. More formally, the R^2 is defined as follows:

$$R^2 = 1 - \frac{\sum_i (y_i - \hat{y})^2}{\sum_i (y_i - \bar{y})^2}$$

where the denominator denotes the total variation, whereas the numerator is the residual sum of squares. Likewise, the MSE is defined as

$$\text{MSE}(\hat{\beta}) = \frac{1}{n} \sum_{i=1}^{n} (y_i - \hat{y})^2$$

```
In [4]: y_pred = reg.predict(X_test)
        e = y_pred-y_test
        print('RMSE:{:.4f}'.format(np.sqrt(mean_squared_error(
                                   y_test,y_pred))))
```

RMSE:4.6387

This result is pretty good but it might be given by chance. As we discussed in Chapter 1, a possible strategy is to implement k-Fold cross validation to validate the model on the data. We split our data on, say, k=10 different Folds. We hold out the first fold, as a test set, and the remaining 9 act as training set. We fit the model on this training set, and evaluate the performance on the test set, obtaining a score. We then hold the second fold as test set, and the remaining 9 folds as training set. We repeat the same process as before, obtaining a new score. We repeat this process for each fold, obtaining then 10 different scores. We then compute the mean of these scores, and we compare it with the score obtained before from the first analysis.

```
In [5]: cv_scores = cross_val_score(reg,X_train, y_train, cv=10)
        print("Average 10-Fold CV Score: {}".format(
                                   (np.mean(cv_scores)) ))
```

Average 10-Fold CV Score: 0.6875346951141157

It looks like the model works pretty well with the Boston dataset. Note that the power of linear model depends on the number of degrees of freedom of the model, that is the number of features we are considering in fitting the model. If the number of samples is large enough (compared to the number of features), then OLS should perform pretty well. However, as the number of features increases, regularized models perform much better.

2.2 Shrinkage Methods

2.2.1 Ridge Regression

Among all unbiased linear techniques, the OLS estimated coefficients are BLUE (Best Linear Unbiased Estimators) with lowest variance, which attains the Cramer-Rao lower bound. However, there is a well known statistical trade-off between variance and bias, so that it is possible to produce models with smaller MSEs by allowing the parameter estimates to be biased. This has an important advantage: by introducing some bias we will obviously loose efficency but we would decrease the test error. Recall that the bias is defined as the difference between the model's average prediction and the true population value, which we aim to predict. In its general terms, the MSE can be therefore rewritten as follows:

$$\text{MSE}(\hat{\beta}) = \text{Var}(\hat{\beta}) + \text{bias}(\beta, \hat{\beta})$$

One method of creating biased regression models is to add a penalty to the sum of the squared errors (SSE). We firsty investigate the *Ridge Regression Model*, which adds a penalty on the sum of the squared regression parameters

$$\min_{\beta \in \mathbb{R}^p} \sum_{i=1}^{p} ||\beta^T \mathbf{x}_i - y_i||^2 + \alpha ||\beta||^2$$

Technically, we have added a penalty, which consists of the squared of the $\mathcal{L}_2$ norm of β; this signifies that a second-order penalty (i.e. the square) is being used on the parameter estimates. The implication of using such norm is that larger values of the parameter estimates are penalized more than smaller values. In effect, this method shrinks the estimates towards 0 as the α penalty becomes large: that's why these techniques are also called shrinkage methods. We expect the coeffcient estimates to be much smaller, in terms of $\mathcal{L}_2$ norm, when a large value of α is used, as compared to when a small value of α is used.

By sacrificing some bias, we can often reduce the variance enough to make the overall MSE lower than unbiased models (such as OLS). The Ridge model makes a trade-off between the simplicity of the model (near-zero coefficients) and its performance on the training set. How much importance the model places on simplicity versus training set performance is specified by α (hyper)-parameter. Increasing α forces the coefficients to move more toward zero, which decreases training set performance but might help generalization (on the test set). Note that by constraining the model, in general, our training performance is worst, but we hope the model will generalize better on the test set. Indeed, if we increase α, model complexity goes down, but the test score should, at least for a while, goes up (or gets better compared to models without regularization).

Regularized models such as the Ridge depends on the hyperparameter α, which should be estimated. A very simple question is: how can we evaluate them? We firtly need to find the optimal value of α that allows us to estimate the model.

Note also that Ridge solutions are not equivalent under scaling of the inputs, so we need to center and scale the predictors so that they are in the same units!

Put in different words, Ridge regression regularizes the linear regression by imposing a penalty on the size of coefficients. Thus the coefficients are shrunk toward zero and toward each other. But when this happens and if the independent variables does not have the same scale, the shrinking is not fair. Two independent variables with different scales will have different contributions to the penalized terms, because the penalized term is a sum of squares of all the coefficients. To avoid such kind of problems, notably, the independent variables are centered and scaled in order to have variance one.

The following code implements the fitting of a Ridge regression model in Python, using the scikit-learn class Ridge .

```
In [6]: ridge = Ridge(normalize=True)
        ridge.fit(X_train, y_train)
        ridge.score(X_test,y_test)
        score = format(ridge.score(X_test,y_test), '.4f')
        print('Ridge Reg Score with Normalization: {}'.format(score))


Ridge Reg Score with Normalization: 0.6241


In [7]: from sklearn.pipeline import make_pipeline, Pipeline
        from sklearn.preprocessing import StandardScaler
        pipe = make_pipeline(StandardScaler(), Ridge())
        pipe.fit(X_train,y_train)
        score_pipe = format(pipe.score(X_test,y_test), '.4f')
        print('Standardized Ridge Score:{}'.format(score_pipe))
```

```
Standardized Ridge Score: 0.7108
```

Numerically, we can see that we have a fair improvement on the estimation of the model (compared to the Linear Regression), but to get a better understanding of the penalty effect on the estimated values, let's plot the shrinkage effect for different values of α's, which shows us the shrinkage effect towards zero of the regression coefficients.

```
In [8]: ridge = Ridge(normalize=True)
        alphas = np.logspace(-3,3,10)
        coef = []
        for a in alphas:
            ridge.set_params(alpha=a)
            ridge.fit(X_train,y_train)
            coef.append(ridge.coef_)
        ax = plt.gca()
        ax.plot(alphas, coef)
        ax.set_xscale('log')
        ax.set_xlim(ax.get_xlim())
        plt.xlabel('$\\alpha$ (alpha)')
        plt.ylabel('Regression Coefficients')
        plt.show()
```

Figure 2.1 shows how the coefficients are shrunk towards zero as α gets bigger. In order to choose the value of α that determines the best model, we cross-validate the solution, that is we look for the value of α that maximizes the R^2, which is by default the score metric in scikit-learn. This is done by performing the GridSearchCV, as follows:

```
In [9]: param_grid = {'alpha': np.logspace(-3,3,10)}
        grid = GridSearchCV(ridge, param_grid, cv=10,
                                     return_train_score=True)
        grid.fit(X_train,y_train)
        best_score = float(format(grid.best_score_, '.4f'))
        print('Best CV score: {:.4f}'.format(grid.best_score_))
        print('Best parameter :',grid.best_params_)
```

```
Best CV score: 0.6887
Best parameter : {'alpha': 0.1}
```

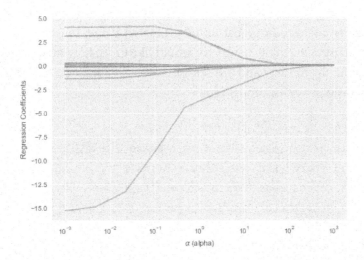

Figure 2.1: Shrinkage effect on the Regression Coefficients in the Boston House Dataset under a $\mathcal{L}_2$-penalty model.

Let's try to fit a series of Ridge regression model for different values of α.

```
In [10]: def ridge_reg(alpha_par):
             ridge = Ridge(alpha=alpha_par, normalize=True)
             ridge.fit(X_train,y_train)
             ridge.predict(X_test)
             score = format(ridge.score(X_test,y_test), '.4f')
             if alpha_par == 'best_score':
                 print('Model with best alpha=', str(alpha_par) +
                 ' has a score equal to ' + str(score))
             else:
                 print('Model with alpha=' + str(alpha_par) +
                 ' has a score equal to ' + str(score))

In [11]: for a in [best_score, 1, 10]:
             ridge_reg(a)

Model with alpha=0.1 has a score equal to 0.6997
Model with alpha=1 has a score equal to 0.6241
Model with alpha=10 has a score equal to 0.2951
```

We see that the model performances drammatically decrease as α gets bigger. The best score for the proposed Ridge model was obtained with the value of $\alpha = 0.1$. Typically, one is interested not just in the estimated value, but also on the uncertanty over that estimate value; hence, we would like to see how much variability we have got on both the training and test sets of the cross-validation folds, and possibly showing the insights with a proper plot.

```python
In [12]: train_scores_mean = grid.cv_results_["mean_train_score"]
         train_scores_std = grid.cv_results_["std_train_score"]
         test_scores_mean = grid.cv_results_["mean_test_score"]
         test_scores_std = grid.cv_results_["std_test_score"]

         plt.figure()
         plt.title('Model Performance')
         plt.xlabel('$\\alpha$ (alpha)')
         plt.ylabel('Score')

         plt.semilogx(alphas, train_scores_mean,
                     label='Mean Train score',color='navy')

         plt.gca().fill_between(alphas,
                               train_scores_mean - train_scores_std,
                               train_scores_mean + train_scores_std,
                               alpha=0.2,
                               color='navy')
         plt.semilogx(alphas, test_scores_mean,
                     label='Mean Test score', color='darkorange')

         plt.gca().fill_between(alphas,
                               test_scores_mean - test_scores_std,
                               test_scores_mean + test_scores_std,
                               alpha=0.2,
                               color='darkorange')

         plt.legend(loc='best')
         plt.show()
```

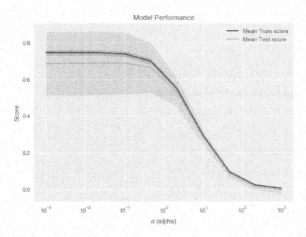

Figure 2.2: Mean Training vs Mean Test score under the Ridge Model for different value of α, with corresponding uncertanty. We see that the uncertanty drammatically reduce its effect after certain values of α, and that the train and test looks very similar, though the train always performs better than the test set, for those values.

2.2.2 Lasso Regression

While Ridge regression shrinks the parameter estimates towards 0, the model does not set the values to absolute 0 for any value of the penalty. Even though some parameter estimates become negligibly small, this model does not conduct feature selection. A popular alternative to Ridge is the *Lasso Regression*, which was introduced by Tibshirani (1996). See also Tibshirani (2013) for a more advanced discussion on the uniqueness of the Lasso solution. This model uses a similar penalty tfo ridge regression:

$$\min_{\beta \in \mathbb{R}^p} \sum_{i=1}^{p} ||\beta^T x_i - y_i||^2 + \alpha ||\beta||_1$$

but differently from that, we are using $\mathcal{L}_1$ norm, which is the sum of absolute values. While the regression coefficients are still shrunk towards zero, differently from $\mathcal{L}_2$ norm, which penalizes more very large coefficients, $\mathcal{L}_1$ penalizes coeffficients equally. In practice, this means that we are basically setting some coefficients equal to zero for some values of α: so this model not only performs regularization to improve the model but it also conducts a sort of feature selection.

In the next snippet, we are going to fit a series of Lasso models for different values of α, and then we append to a new list all the estimated coefficients.

```
In [13]:  lasso = Lasso(max_iter=10000,normalize=True)
          coefs = list()
          for alpha in alphas:
              lasso.set_params(alpha=alpha)
              lasso.fit(X_train,y_train)
              coefs.append(lasso.coef_)
          ax = plt.gca()
          ax.plot(alphas, coefs)
          ax.set_xscale('log')
          ax.set_xlim(ax.get_xlim())
          plt.xlabel('$\\alpha$ (alpha)')
          plt.ylabel('Regression Coefficients')
          plt.show()
```

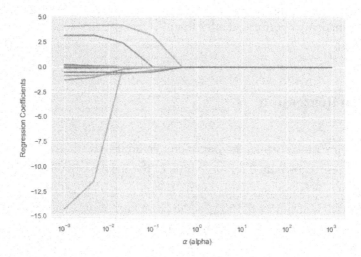

Figure 2.3: Shrinkage effect on the Regression Coefficients using a Lasso Penalization.

Typically, one resorts to Lasso regression because it shrinks some of the coefficients to zero, which litterally translates into feature selection. We implent this method afain on the Boston House dataset, and see which features seem to be relevant for the prediction of the median house price.

```
In [14]:  names = df.drop('MEDV', axis=1).columns
          lasso = Lasso(alpha=0.1, normalize=True)
          lasso_coef = lasso.fit(X, y).coef_
```

```
_ = plt.plot(range(len(names)), lasso_coef)
_ = plt.xticks(range(len(names)), names, rotation=60)
_ = plt.ylabel('Coefficients')
plt.show()
```

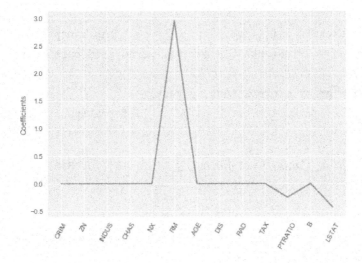

Figure 2.4: Feature Importance in Lasso regression.

Lasso's coefficients most important predictors have values different from zero, whereas the others are shrunk to zero. This is very important procedure for any machine learning model, since it allows you to communicate a numerical result in terms of important factors that affect the dependent variable.

2.2.3 Elastic Net

A generalization of the lasso model is the Elastic Net, introduced by Zou and Hastie (2005), which combines both $\mathcal{L}_1$ and $\mathcal{L}_2$ penalties together:

$$\min_{\beta \in \mathbb{R}^p} \sum_{i=1}^{p} ||\beta^T x_i - y_i||^2 + \alpha_1 ||\beta||_1 + \alpha_2 ||\beta||_2^2$$

In scikit-learn, it is parametrized differently

$$\min_{\beta \in \mathbb{R}^p} \sum_{i=1}^{p} ||\beta^T x_i - y_i||^2 + \alpha \, \eta \, ||\beta||_1 + \alpha \, (1 - \eta) \, ||\beta||_2^2$$

where η captures the relative amount of $\mathcal{L}_1$-penalty.

```
In [15]: steps = [('scaler', StandardScaler()),
                  ('elasticnet', ElasticNet())]

        pipeline = Pipeline(steps)

        parameters = {'elasticnet__l1_ratio': np.linspace(0, 1, 30)}
        gm_cv = GridSearchCV(pipeline, param_grid=parameters)
        gm_cv.fit(X_train, y_train)
        r2 = gm_cv.score(X_test, y_test)
        print("Tuned ElasticNet Alpha: {}".format(gm_cv.best_params_))
        print("Tuned ElasticNet R squared: {}".format(r2))
```

```
Tuned ElasticNet Alpha: {'elasticnet__l1_ratio': 0.9310}
Tuned ElasticNet R squared: 0.6441
```

2.3   Robust Regression

```
In [16]: from sklearn.linear_model import LinearRegression,
                             HuberRegressor, RANSACRegressor
        from sklearn import datasets
        import numpy as np
        from matplotlib import pyplot as plt
```

The models we have investigated so far are, by construction, sensitive to outliers. In standard statistics, an outlier can be defined in several ways, but in general, an outlier is an example that differs significantly from other observations in the sample. In particular, when it is reasonable to assume that the sample comes from a Normal distribution, a popular way to detect outliers is by means of the *empirical rule*, which basically says that approximately 68% of the observations lies between one standard deviation σ from the mean. With this idea, we typically identify outliers as examples which are extreme events in this distribution, say above $\pm 3\sigma$.

But why are linear models sensitive to outliers? All the methods we have investigated so far minimize an objective function which is based on the residual sum of squares, and therefore every single point in the fit contribute to this objective cost function. To overcome to this potential problem, Robust Regression provides a valide alternative to standard linear models, and are particularly suggested when we suspect to have either outliers in the sample or heteroscedasticity in the model.

In particular, since outliers tend to significantly impact the OLS fitting estimation procedure by affecting the slope of the fitting curve, Robust Regression models, instead, reduce the influence of outliers, making easier the outliers detection.

Here, we will introduce a couple methods that allow the fit of robust regression, namely the Huber Regression and the RANdom SAmple Consensus (RANSAC), poposed by Huber (1964) and Fischler and Bolles (1981), respectively. The interested reader might refer to the book by Andersen (2008) for further details and different methodologies on this issue.

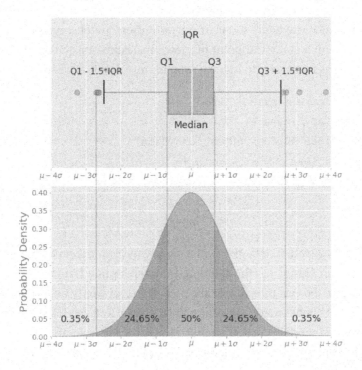

Figure 2.5 Empirical rule in action: outliers notably are identified as extreme events in this distribution.

2.3.1   Huber Regression

This method was proposed by Peter Huber in 1964, and it extends the stadard OLS by introducing a loss that is less sensitive to outliers when the raw output model (i.e. the difference between the observed and predicted value) is too large. In particular, this is achieved by introducing a loss that is a piecewise function that optimizes either the squared loss or absolute loss for the samples based on a parameter, denoted by ϵ, which basically controls the number of outliers impacting the fit. More formally, we wish to minimize the following cost function:

$$\min_{\beta} \sum_{i=1}^{n} L\left(y_i, f(x_i)\right)$$

where

$$L(y, f(x)) = \begin{cases} (y - f(x))^2 & \text{if } |y - f(x)| < \epsilon \\ 2 \cdot \epsilon \cdot |y - f(x)| & \text{otherwise} \end{cases}$$

Hence, the Huber loss function is squared for small prediction errors, and linear for larger values, which are likely to occur when outliers are observed. This is shown in Figure 2.6. From a statistical point of view, this estimator belongs to the class of M-estimators, which is a way to identify Maximum Likelihood Estimators.

```
In [17]: plt.figure(figsize=(8,5))
         data = np.linspace(-20, 20)
         huber_loss = plots.huber_loss(data)
         squared_loss =  0.5 * data ** 2
         plots.plot_loss_(data, huber_loss, squared_loss,
                     'Huber Loss', 'Squared Loss',
                     'Huber $\epsilon=3$', 'OLS')
```

For the sake of illustration, let's try to fit a simple OLS model on a dataset with outliers. As shown in Figure 2.7, the estiamted model is pulled down by the bunch of outliers, shown in the east direction of the plot. Here, we apply twice the customized function called fit_huber, which basically fits a Huber Regressor and returns the estimated regression model. We see, again from Figure 2.7, that an $\epsilon \to 1$ produces a model that forgets the outliers, wherever the model tends to get closer to the OLS estimator as this parameter gets bigger.

```
In [18]: def fit_Huber(X,y,epsilon):
             huber = HuberRegressor(epsilon=epsilon)
             huber.fit(X, y)
             coef_huber = huber.coef_ *X + huber.intercept_
             return coef_huber

         def fit_OLS(X,y):
```

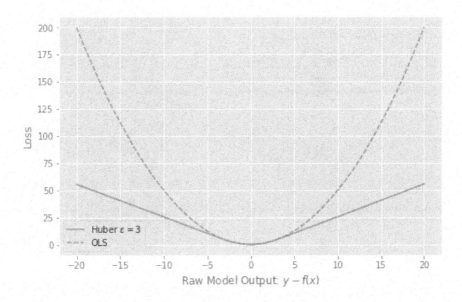

Figure 2.6: Different behaviour of the Squared vs Huber Loss for increasing values in the model prediction residuals.

```
lr = LinearRegression()
lr.fit(X, y)
coef_lr = lr.coef_ *X + lr.intercept_
return coef_lr
```

In [19]: X, y, coef = datasets.make_regression(n_samples=800,
                                    n_features=1,
                                    n_informative=1,
                                    noise=10, coef=True,
                                    random_state=0)

```
n_outliers = 50
X[:n_outliers] = 3 + 0.5*np.random.normal(size=(n_outliers,1))
y[:n_outliers] = -3 + 10*np.random.normal(size=n_outliers)

ols = fit_OLS(X,y)
huber1 = fit_Huber(X,y,epsilon=1.5)
huber2 = fit_Huber(X,y,epsilon=3)
```

In [20]: plt.figure(figsize=(8,5))

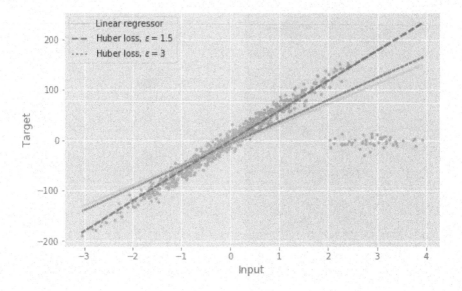

Figure 2.7: Fitting of a standard OLS and Huber Regression in the presence of outliers.

```
plt.scatter(X,y,color='yellowgreen', marker='.')
plt.plot(X, ols, label='Linear regressor',
        color='gold', linestyle='solid', linewidth=2)
plt.plot(X, huber1, label="Huber loss, $\epsilon=1.5$",
        color='green', linestyle='dashed', linewidth=2)
plt.plot(X, huber2, label="Huber loss, $\epsilon=3$",
        color='red', linestyle='dotted', linewidth=2 )
plt.legend(loc='upper left')
plt.xlabel("Input")
plt.ylabel("Target")
plt.show()
```

2.3.2   RANSAC

RANSAC is not properly a statistical model but an iterative algorithm, developed in 1981, which turns out to be extremely consistent to outliers. It basically divides the available data into two different subsets, namely outlier and inlier. The latter subset is also denoted as the hypothetical inliers. The hypothetical inliers are used to fit the model, whereas the former group is then used to compute the residuals errors. All the points that stick to the model prediction are grouped to form the *consensus set*. RANSAC algorithm continues iterating until the consensus set is large enough for the fitting to be consistent with respect to outliers. The following snippet contains a custom function, called fit_RANSAC that returns the predicted model: results of the fitting on this synthetic dataset is shown in Figure 2.8.

```
In [21]: def fit_RANSAC(X,y):
             """
             This Function fits a RANSAC Regressor and returns
             the (best) fitted model, as well as the ordered X.
             The function also returns the set of inliers and
             outliers on which the model was fitted"""

             rc = RANSACRegressor()
             rc.fit(X, y)
             yhat = rc.predict(X)
             pred = rc.estimator_.coef_*X + rc.estimator_.intercept_
             return pred


         ransac=fit_RANSAC(X,y)

In [22]: plt.figure(figsize=(8,5))
         plt.scatter(X,y,color='yellowgreen', marker='.')
         plt.plot(X, ols, label='Linear regressor',
                 color='gold', linestyle='solid', linewidth=2)
         plt.plot(X, huber1, label="Huber loss, $\epsilon=1.5$",
                 color='green',linestyle='dotted', linewidth=2)
         plt.plot(X, ransac,label='RANSAC regressor',
                 color='cornflowerblue', linestyle='dashed', linewidth=2)
         plt.legend(loc='upper left')
         plt.xlabel("Input")
         plt.ylabel("Target")
         plt.show()
```

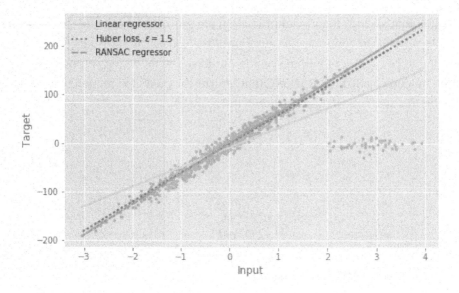

Figure 2.8: Huber vs RANSAC Regression (under the OLS baseline).

2.4   Logistic Regression

The difference between regression and classification problems is that in the former, the real focus is on the estimation of a continuous response, while in the latter, we are just interested in the sign of the prediction, that is if a specific example belongs to a class or not. In particular, we are interested in how well your model performs on prediction. We want to optimize this procedure by finding β (and b in case of presence of intercept) that minimizes the number of missclassification. But what do we mean with missclassification? In terms of loss functions, regression models typically minimize the squared errors, but if we assume that the target value is one (as in binary classification), then such quadratic loss penalizes large deviations from it. This argument is not appealing for classification: being close to the true value does not mean anything in classfication problems, since we are interested in correctly classifying the test examples in the correct class.

We could think of using the so-called $0 - 1$ loss, which takes the sum of incorrect missclassification. Given an example, if we correctly predict, then the loss is zero, otherwise is one. Unfortunately, such function is hard to minimize (i.e. it is not convex and even not continuous), so we might think of using a smoother version of such loss function, which is used in logistic regression, called log-loss function, defined as

$$\sum_{i=1}^{n} \log \left(\exp(-y_i \beta^T x_i) + 1 \right)$$

2.4.1 Why Logistic Regression is Linear?

In any binary classification problem, the aim is to predict a binary outcome $y = \{0, 1\}$ given a set of independent features. When a binary outcome variable is modeled using logistic regression, it is assumed that the logit transformation of the outcome variable has a linear relationship with the predictor variables. To see this, we could think of using $\hat{y} = \beta^T x + b$ as a predictor of y. This could be a reasonable choice, especially when the outcome is continuous, that is $\hat{y} \in (-\infty, \infty)$. However, in binary classification the outcome is discrete, that is $y = \{0, 1\}$, and so choosing such (linear) function to predict y is not good for our purposes. However, we could think of applying the logistic function (also called sigmoid function), which takes any real input $t \in \mathbb{R}$, and outputs a value between $[0, 1]$, that is

$$\sigma(t) = \frac{1}{(1 + e^{-t})}$$

Since we want to predict which class the example belongs to, based on the observed features, we could think of using a linear combination of the features as classifier, that is $\beta^T x$. Then, the sigmoid function becomes

$$\mathbb{P}(Y = 1) = \sigma\left(\beta^T x\right) = \frac{1}{\left(1 + e^{-\beta^T x}\right)}$$

Thanks to this function, we are able to map $\hat{y}$ from $(-\infty, \infty)$ to $[0, 1]$, and to give a probabilistic interpretation to any binary classification problem.

In Logistic Regression, we want $\mathbb{P}(Y = 1)$ to be high, so we need to choose β so that it minimizes the log-loss function on the training dataset, that is

$$\min_{\beta \in \mathbb{R}^p} - \sum_{i=1}^{n} \log \left(\exp(-y_i \beta^T x_i) + 1 \right)$$

Hence, Logistic Regression is linear because the outcome depends on the raw output model, that is $\beta^T x$, and produces a linear decision surface for each value of x such

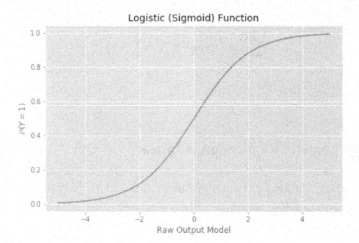

Figure 2.9: Theoretical Logistic Function, with threshold set to 0.5

that

$$\frac{1}{1 + e^{\beta^T x}} = 0.5 \quad \Longleftrightarrow \quad \beta^T x = 0$$

However, the logistic function is not linear at all. To see this, consider the inverse of the logistic function, called the logit, which is the log of the odds ratio.

Consider the ratio of the probabilities with which a certain training example x belongs to the class $y = 1$ and to the class $y = 0$, that is

$$\frac{\mathbb{P}\left(y = 1 \mid x\right)}{\mathbb{P}\left(y = 0 \mid x\right)} = e^{\beta^T x}$$

Then, taking the log on both sides yields to

$$\log \left(\frac{\mathbb{P}\left(y = 1 \mid x\right)}{\mathbb{P}\left(y = 0 \mid x\right)} \right) = \beta^T x$$

which illustrates that the logit - i.e. the log-odds or natural logarithm of the odds - is equivalent to the linear regression expression.

2.4.2   Logistic Regression Predictions (Raw Model Output) vs Probabilities (Sigmoid Output)

Logistic regression is useful when one wants to give a probabilistic interpretation of the classification problem. Since the decision boundary is given by the plane $\beta^T x$, then, for a specific training example, if the raw model output is positive, then we predict one, otherwise zero, that is

$$\text{raw model output: } \beta^T x[i] > 0 \Rightarrow \text{prediction class is } 1$$

$$\text{raw model output: } \beta^T x[i] < 0 \Rightarrow \text{prediction class is } 0$$

The sigmoid function squashes the raw model output in probabilities: the more we move away from the boundaries, the more confident the prediction. Hence,

$$\mathbb{P}\left(Y = 1 | x\right) = \sigma\left(\beta^T x\right) = \frac{1}{\left(1 + e^{-\beta^T x}\right)} = \begin{cases} \geq 0.5 & \hat{y} = 1 \\ < 0.5 & \hat{y} = 0 \end{cases}$$

This function just compute the probability of correctly classifying the traning example, and hence we tend to use the Logistic Regression if one wants to get probabilities rather than raw output model.

2.4.3 Logistic Regression in Python

```
In [23]: from egeaML import DataIngestion
         from egeaML import classification_plots
         from sklearn.linear_model import LogisticRegression
         from sklearn.metrics import classification_report
         from sklearn.metrics import roc_auc_score, roc_curve
```

In order to illustrate how Logistic Regression model works, we use the Diabetes dataset, which is available on the repository of this book on GitHub. Let's read the data and store it into a pandas DataFrame. We then separate the target variable, which is a dummy variable describing whether the disease was observed or not, from the independent variables, and split them into train and test set. As usual, we make use of the book-specific class DataIngestion.

```
In [24]: r = DataIngestion(df='diabetes.csv', col_target = 'diabetes')
         data = r.load_data()
         X = r.features()
         y = r.target()
         X_train, X_test, y_train, y_test = train_test_split(X,y, \
                     test_size=0.3, random_state=42)
```

Fitting a Logistic Regression Model is pretty straighforward in scikit-learn:

```
In [25]: lr = LogisticRegression()
         lr.fit(X_train,y_train)
         y_pred = lr.predict(X_test)
         print('Prediction:', lr.predict(X_test)[1],\
               lr.predict(X_test)[9],lr.predict(X_test)[25])
         print('Raw Model Output X_test:', \
               (lr.coef_@ X_test[1] + lr.intercept_),
               (lr.coef_@ X_test[9] + lr.intercept_),
               (lr.coef_@ X_test[25] + lr.intercept_))
```

```
Prediction: 0 1 1
Raw Model Output X_test: [-1.24489634] [0.73742309] [1.27685211]
```

We can obtain the hard probabilities in Logistic regression by applying the predict_proba() method. This function returns the probability of a given example being in a particular class; in other words, it returns a vector, where the first column describes the probability the training example belongs to the first class, the second column describes the probability the example belongs to the second class, and so on (for multiclass problems). We implement this function in the first two training examples, and the result is shown.

```
In [26]: lr.predict_proba(X_test)[:2]
```

```
Out[26]: array([[0.66557856, 0.33442144],
                [0.77641514, 0.22358486]])
```

The classifier is reporting over 66% and 77% confidence probability being in the 0-class for the first and second training example, respectively. This is consistent with the prediction we obtained with the predict() method.

2.4.4   Model Performance Evaluation

In classification problems, we typically evaluate model performance with accuracy, defined as the fraction of correct predictions. Without loss of generality, let us consider a binary classification problem. To evaluate the performance of the choosen model, we typically resort to the confusion matrix, which is shown in Figure 2.10. More formally, the accuracy on the test set of the trained model is obtained as

$$accuracy = \frac{TP + TN}{TP + TN + FP + FN}$$

where $TP + TN$ is the sum of the diagonal matrix, and TP is called True Positive and TN is called True Negative. An example is said to be a

- True Positive if it was predicted as positive, given that it actually belongs to the positive class;

- False Positive if it was predicted as positive, given that it actually belongs to the 0-class;

- False Negative if it was predicted as zero, given that it actually belongs to the positive class;

- True Negative if it was predicted as zero, given that it actually belongs to the 0-class.

In general, we would like to minimize the number of False Negative (FN) and maximize the number of True Positive (TP), but that depends on the use case under investigation. However, accuracy is not a good metric when the problem under investigation is characterized by imbalanced classes, that is when one class in much more frequent than the other: this is, for instance, the case when one deals with fraud detection. Indeed, fraudsters are (luckily) just a small, yet relevant, percentage among the observed statistical units, and therefore the model might face some difficulties in spotting a positive case among the many negative ones. See Section 1.3 for details on how to deal with imbalanced datasets.

Hence, from the confusion matrix, we can retrive other metrics, such as the precision defined as

$$\text{precision} = \frac{TP}{TP + FP}$$

and the recall (also known as True Positive Rate, TPR) defined as

$$\text{recall} = \frac{TP}{TP + FN}$$

Practically speaking, high precision transaltes into the observations of a high number of TP and not many FP - i.e. not many fraudsters were classified as non fraudsters - whereas high recall means most fraudsters were correctly predicted.

```
In [27]: labels = ['Healthy', 'Diabetes']
         classification_plots.confusion_matrix(y_test, y_pred,
                                    cmap="Blues",
                                    xticklabels=labels,
                                    yticklabels=labels)
```

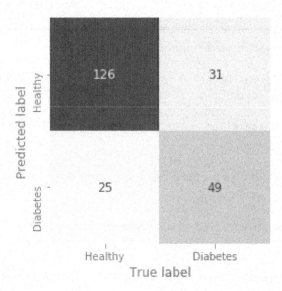

Figure 2.10: Confusion Matrix for the Diabetes Dataset on the Test set.

Note that there exists a relevant trade-off between precision and recall, whioch is shown in Figure 2.11, produced by the book-specific function plot_precision_recall in the following snippet:

```
In [28]: classification_plots.plot_precision_recall(y_test, y_pred)
```

To overcome to this problem, it is frequently used an alternative score, called F1 score, which is defined as the harmonic mean of precision and recall

$$\text{F1-score} = 2 \cdot \frac{\text{precision} \cdot \text{recall}}{\text{precision} + \text{recall}}$$

The three metrics can be shown altogether using the classification_report provided by the scikit-learn library.

```
In [29]: print(classification_report(y_test, y_pred))

             precision    recall  f1-score   support

          0       0.80      0.83      0.82       151
          1       0.66      0.61      0.64        80

avg / total       0.75      0.76      0.76       231
```

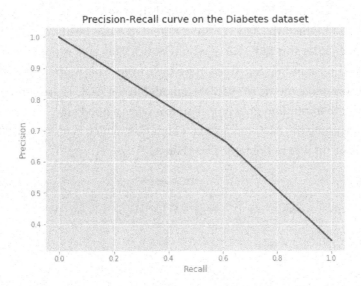

Figure 2.11: Precision-Recall Curve on the Diabetes Dataset.

Classification reports and confusion matrices are great methods to quantitatively evaluate model performances, especially when we deal with multiclass classification problems. However, in many situations, we might prefer using the Receiver Operating Characteristics (ROC) curve, which provides a way to visually evaluate models. To construct the ROC curve, we will compute the predicted probabilities from the predict_proba() method, and we will consider only the second column of the array. This is because the first column of the predict_proba() method contains the probability of being classified in the 0-class, while the second in the 1-class.

```
In [30]: y_pred_proba = lr.predict_proba(X_test)[:,1]
         fpr, tpr, threshold = roc_curve(y_test, y_pred_proba)
         plt.plot([0, 1], [0, 1], 'k--')
         plt.plot(fpr, tpr)
         plt.xlabel('False Positive Rate')
         plt.ylabel('True Positive Rate')
         plt.title('ROC Curve')
         plt.show()
```

How can we interpret Figure 2.12? Given the ROC curve, can we extract a metric of interest? The larger the area under the ROC, the better the model. In other words, say you have a binary classifier that in fact is just randomly making guesses. It would be correct approximately 50% of the time, and the resulting ROC curve would be a diagonal line in which the True Positive Rate and False Positive Rate are always equal. The area under this ROC curve would be 0.5. This area is notably denoted by the acronym AUC, standing for Area Under the Curve. This is one way in which the AUC is an informative metric to evaluate a model. If the AUC is greater than 0.5, the model is better than random guessing. This is always a good sign.

We can also compute the AUC using cross validation, which is useful when we want to be sure the result was not obtained by chance.

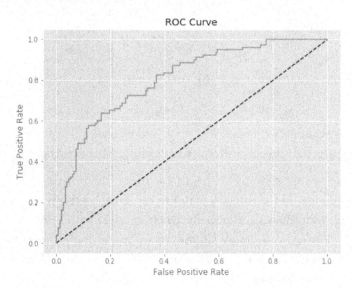

Figure 2.12: The Receiver operating characteristic (ROC) Curve

```
In [31]: roc_auc_score = roc_auc_score(y_test, y_pred_proba)
         cv_scores =cross_val_score(lr,X,y,cv=10,scoring='roc_auc')
         print('ROC AUC Score:{:.4f}'.format(roc_auc_score))
         print('ROC AUC Score using Cross Validation: {:.4f}'.format(
                                              np.mean(cv_scores)))

ROC AUC Score:0.8059
ROC AUC Score using Cross Validation: 0.8246
```

2.4.5 Regularization

In Logistic Regression, we apply an $\mathcal{L}_2$ regularization by default, in the same way that Ridge does for regression. $\mathcal{L}_1$-Regularization is anyway possible, which is appealing for feature selection.

Differently from Ridge, we have an hyperparameter $C = \frac{1}{\alpha}$, so that smaller C means more regularization. More regularization penalize large coefficients, which has the effect of of making the training accuracy going down but improves the test accuracy. Also recall that $\mathcal{L}_1$ performs feature selection (some coefficients are set to zero), whereas $\mathcal{L}_2$ shrinks coefficients to be smaller.

Regularization is useful in high dimensional space, and the Logistic regression problem can be rewritten (in terms of loss function) as

$$\min_{\beta \in \mathbb{R}^p} -C \sum_{i=1}^{n} \log\left(\exp(-y_i \beta^T x_i) + 1\right) + ||\beta||_2^2 \qquad \mathcal{L}_2 - norm$$

$$\min_{\beta \in \mathbb{R}^p} -C \sum_{i=1}^{n} \log\left(\exp(-y_i \beta^T x_i) + 1\right) + ||\beta||_1 \qquad \mathcal{L}_1 - norm$$

To fit a Logistic Regression model under the $\mathcal{L}_1$-penalty, we just need to add the argument penalty equal to $\mathcal{L}_1$.

```
In [32]: lr_l1 = LogisticRegression(penalty='l1')
         lr_l2 = LogisticRegression()
         lr_l1.fit(X_train, y_train)
         lr_l2.fit(X_train,y_train)
         print(round(lr_l1.score(X_test,y_test),2) )
         print(round(lr_l2.score(X_test,y_test),2) )


0.7446
0.7576
```

The above code shows two Logistic Regression models without specifying the regularization parameter C. We implement GridSearchCV to look up for the best C which produces the best score on the train set.

```
In [33]: c_space = np.logspace(-5, 8, 15)
         param_grid = {'C': c_space,'penalty': ['l1', 'l2']}
         logreg = LogisticRegression()
         logreg_cv = GridSearchCV(logreg, param_grid, cv=5)
         logreg_cv.fit(X_train,y_train)
         print("Tuned Logistic Reg Parameters: {}".format(
                         logreg_cv.best_params_))
         print("Best Train score is {}".format(
```

```
                                    logreg_cv.best_score_))
        print("Best Test score is {}".format(
                                    logreg_cv.score(X_test,y_test)))
```

```
Tuned Logistic Reg Parameters: {'C': 3.727593720314938}
Best Train score is 0.7746741154562383
Best Test score is 0.7445887445887446
```

```
Tuned Logistic Reg Parameter: {'C': 31.622776601683793,'penalty': '12'}
Tuned Logistic Reg Accuracy: 0.7673913043478261
```

Note that in Logistic Regression, all points contribute to β: if you leave out any point of your data, that will change the solution. However, that is not true for Support Vector Machine (SVM), which is discussed in the following Section.

2.5   Linear Support Vector Machine

We talked about Logistic Regression, which is a linear classifier learned with a logistic loss function. Linear SVM are also linear classifiers but they use Hinge loss instead of the log-loss. Broadly speaking, the log-loss is sometime viewed as the smoothed version of the Hinge loss, and Figure 2.13 shows the difference between the two losses: this was produced with the book-specific methos plot_loss from the plots class.

```
In [34]: from egeaML import functions_utils,plots,classification_plots
         from sklearn.datasets.samples_generator import make_blobs
         import mglearn
         from sklearn.svm import SVC
         import numpy as np

In [35]: data = np.linspace(-3,3,1000)
         utils = functions_utils(data)
         logistic_loss = utils.logistic_loss()
         hinge_loss = utils.hinge_loss()
         plots.plot_loss(data, logistic_loss, hinge_loss
                     ,'Logistic Loss', 'Hinge Loss'
                     ,'Logistic', 'Hinge'
                     ,xlim=[-3,3], ylim=[-0.05, 5])
```

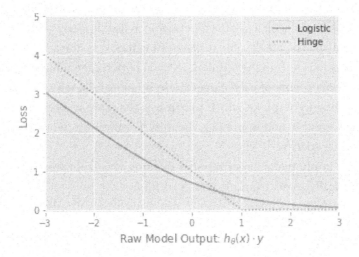

Figure 2.13: Plots of common Classification Loss Functions: on the y-axis, we have the loss, whereas on the x-axis we have the raw-model output.

They look very similar, but if a training example falls in the 0-loss Hinge region (right), it doesn't contribute to the fit. If we remove it, nothing will change; points that, instead, are in the 1-loss region are called *Support Vectors*: we then say that Support Vectors are examples that are not in the flat part of the loss diagram, i.e. that have no 0-loss.

In other words, support vectors are examples that are incorrectly classified or close to the boundary. How close these points are to the boundary plane is controlled by regularization strength: if an example is not a support vector, removing it has no effect on the model. This is a key property of Support Vector Machines: just a few points contribute to the solution, whereas in Logistic Regression, all points matter to the fit because there is no 0-loss flat region in the loss.

Linear SVM looks for the hyperplane that maximizes the margins for linearly separable data (and minimizes the number of missclassification in case we have overlapping classes). The margin is defined as the distance from the boundary to the closest points of each class. Mathematically, the aim is to choose β that minimize the Hinge loss, that is

$$\min_{\beta \in \mathbb{R}^p} \left[C \sum_{i=1}^{n} \max\left\{0, 1 - y_i \beta^T x_i\right\} + \frac{||\beta||^2}{2} \right]$$

In order to minimize the Hinge loss, we need to have large values of decision function $\beta^T x_i$, which happens when points are far off on the correct side of the decision boundary. This is saying that $\beta^T x_i$ should have the same sign as y_i, so if their product is positive, then we get a loss of zero, else it increases linearly with $\beta^T x$ when the product is negative. The smaller the decision function $\beta^T x_i$, the larger the loss.

In practice, the aim is to find the optimal decision hyperplane which is as far as possible from the data points of each category. In other words, we are looking for the optimal separating hyperplane which maximizes the margin (between the training points for class 1 and 0) and minimizes the missclassification (when the two classes overlap in feature space).

Larger margins imply that a larger number of support vectors are considered in the fit. More specifically, every example which is either

- inside the margins or

- every example that is outside the margins but missclassified

contribute to the solution, and these points are called support vectors. Note that the size of the margins is basically the inverse of the length of β, so smaller values means larger margins. Support vectors are therefore points which have non-zero loss and close to the boundary.

We create a toy dataset using the scikit-learn function make_ blobs: its argument centers controls the clusters to be created, that is centers= 2 will produce two different clouds of points. We also plot the data: note that the argument $s = 50$ determines the size of the balls, whereas $c = y$ colors the balls according to the y values

```
In [36]: X, y = make_blobs(n_samples=100, centers=2,n_features=2,
                    random_state=3, cluster_std=1.1)


         plt.scatter(X[:, 0], X[:, 1], c=y, s=50,  cmap='winter')
         plt.xlabel('Feature 0')
         plt.ylabel('Feature 1')
         plt.show()
```

When there is no overlapping between the two classes (as in the above case), SVM aims to find the optimal decision boundary that maximizes the margin. In particular, maximizing the margin is equivalent to minimizing the length of β, since the margin is the inverse of the length of β.

```
In [37]: X_train, X_test, y_train, y_test = train_test_split(X,
                    y, test_size=0.3, random_state=42)
         svc = SVC(kernel='linear')
```

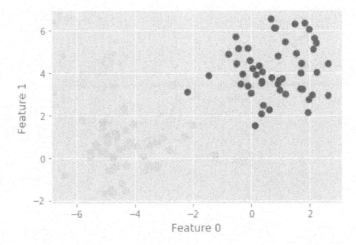

Figure 2.14: Scatter Plot of the toy data used for the illustration of the SVM.

```
svc.fit(X_train, y_train)
pred = svc.predict(X_test)
print(svc.score(X_test, y_test))
```

1.0

We now show the decision boundaries obtained from the SVC, using the book-specific function plot_svc_decision_function: this function identifies the decision boundaries that maximizes the margins, as well as the support vectors.

```
In [38]: plt.scatter(X[:, 0], X[:, 1], c=y, s=50, cmap='winter')
         classification_plots.plot_svc_decision_function(svc)
         sv = svc.support_vectors_
         sv_labels= svc.dual_coef_.ravel()>0
         mglearn.discrete_scatter(sv[:,0], sv[:,1], sv_labels, s=10,
                                  markeredgewidth=1.5)
         plt.xlabel('Feature 0')
         plt.ylabel('Feature 1')
         plt.show()
```

This is the dividing line that maximizes the margins between the two sets of points. Note that a few of the training points just touch the margin: these points are the pivotal elements of this fit, that is the *support vectors*.

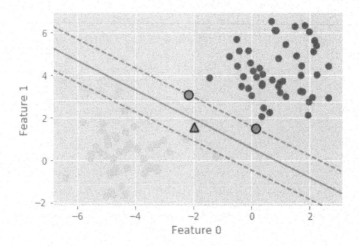

Figure 2.15: Identification of the Decision Boundaries and Support Vectors.

```
In [39]: svc.support_vectors_

Out[39]: array([[-2.19135348,   3.0939319 ],
                 [ 0.13181535,   1.50196496],
                 [-1.99456657,   1.53111627]])
```

Regarding the fit, it is worth to notice that only the position of the support vectors matters: any correctly classified point further from the margin does not modify the fit. Technically, this is because these points do not contribute to the loss function used to fit the model, so their position and value do not matter as long as they do not cross the margin.

The dataset we have just used basically describes a case when data is linearly separable, that is when a perfect decision boundary exists. But what if the data has some amount of overlap? In such cases, SVM looks for the hyperplane that maximizes the margin and minimizes the missclassification. For example, consider the data like the one in Figure 2.16:

```
In [40]: X, y = make_blobs(n_samples=100, centers=2, random_state=0,
                           cluster_std=1.2)
         plt.scatter(X[:, 0], X[:, 1], c=y, s=50, cmap='winter')
         plt.show()
```

A possible strategy to use in this case is to introduce a penalty term, which allows some points to fall out the margin, at the cost of penalizing them. The name *soft-*

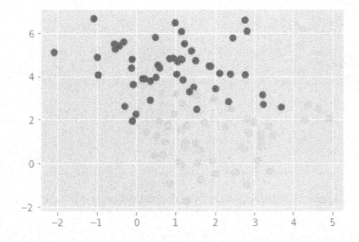

Figure 2.16: Scatter Plot of a overlapping, two-classes, dataset.

margins comes from this penalization method. The hardness of the margin is controlled by a tuning parameter, denoted by C, which is the inverse of α, used to denote the regularization parameter in Linear Regression. There is an interesting aspect of how the parameter C acts. Using low values of C will cause the algorithm to try to adjust to the majority of data points, while using a higher value of C stresses the importance of each individual data point. In other words,

- Under low regularization (i.e. for large C), the margins are tight, and points cannot lie in it, and therefore few support vectors.

- Under high regularization (i.e. for smaller C,) the margins are softer, and therefore more support vectors, which influence the solution.

This is shown in the Figure 2.17, generated from the following snippet.

```
In [41]: classification_plots.plot_svc_regularization_effect(X=X,y=y,
                         kernel='linear',cmap='winter')
```

The interest reader can refer to the book by Muller and Guido (2017) to deepen her curiosity on the regularization effect on the decision boundaries.

2.6   Beyond Linearity: Kernelized Models

Where SVM becomes extremely powerful is when it is combined with kernels. To motivate the use of kernels, let us look at some data that is not linearly separable.

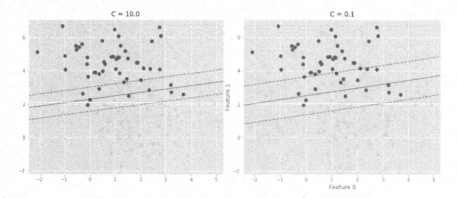

Figure 2.17: Effect on the regularization on the margins.

```
In [42]: from sklearn.datasets.samples_generator import make_circles
         X, y = make_circles(100, factor=.1, noise=.1)
         clf = SVC(kernel='linear').fit(X, y)
         plt.scatter(X[:, 0], X[:, 1], c=y, s=50, cmap='winter')
         classification_plots.plot_svc_decision_function(clf,
                         plot_support=False)
         plt.show()
```

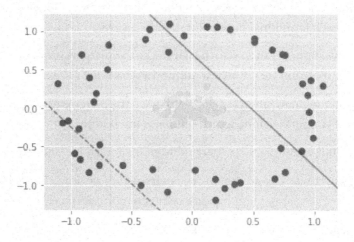

Figure 2.18: A Linear Hyperplane with non-linear data is not feasible.

Using a linear hyperplane to separate these two classes is not feasible. However, we could think of projecting the data into a higher dimension such that a linear separator would be sufficient. How can we achieve this? By simply adding a new set of features, obtained from the original ones. For instance, instead of representing each data point as a two-dimensional point, (x_0, x_1), we now represent it as a three-dimensional point, (x_0, x_1, x_1^2). The message here is that adding nonlinear features to the representation of our data can make linear models much more powerful. However, often we do not know which features to add, and adding many features (like all possible interactions in a 100-dimensional feature space) might make computations very expensive.

Luckily, there is a clever mathematical trick that allows us to learn a classifier in a higher-dimensional space without actually computing the new, possibly very large representation. This is known as *kernel trick*, and it works by directly computing the distance (more precisely, the scalar products) of the data points for the exapanded feature representation, without ever actually computing the expansion.

There are two ways to map the data into a higher-dimensional space that are commonly used with SVM:

- the polynomial kernel, which computes all possible polynomials up to a certain degree of the original features, such as $(x_0^2 \cdot x_1^5)$;

- the radial basis function (RBF) kernel, also known as Gaussian kernel: intuitively, it considers all possible polynomials of all degress, but the importance of the features decreases for higher degrees.

```
In [43]: clf = SVC(kernel='rbf', C=1E6)
         clf.fit(X,y)
         plt.scatter(X[:,0],X[:,1],c=y,s=50, cmap='winter')
         classification_plots.plot_svc_decision_function(clf)
         plt.scatter(clf.support_vectors_[:,0],
                     clf.support_vectors_[:,1],
                     s=300,lw=1, facecolors='none')
         sv = clf.support_vectors_
         sv_labels= clf.dual_coef_.ravel()>0
         mglearn.discrete_scatter(sv[:,0], sv[:,1], sv_labels,
             s=10, markeredgewidth=1.5)
         plt.xlabel('Feature 0')
         plt.ylabel('Feature 1')
         plt.show()
```

Using this kernelized SVM with radial basis function, we have learned a suitable nonlinear decision boundary for this dataset.

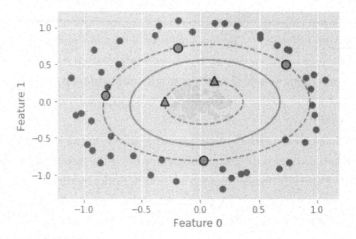

Figure 2.19: Fitting a SVM to non-linear data using the Kernel Trick produces non-linear decision boundaries.

2.6.1   Into the Hood of the Kernel Trick

Suppose that at the optimum, the β can be written as linear combination of the data points, that is

$$\beta = \sum_{i=1}^{n} \alpha_i x_i$$

where the α's are called the *dual coefficients*, and they are non-zero only for points which contribute to the solution. There is an important relationship between α's and C such that $\alpha_i \leq C$ for each training example i, that is C limits the influence of each data point. Note that

$$\hat{y} = \sigma(\beta^T x) \Rightarrow \hat{y} = \sigma\left(\sum_i \alpha_i \left(x_i^T x\right)\right)$$

The idea of this rewriting is that now the solution and the prediction problem can be expressed in terms of the inner product $x_i^T x$. Suppose we want to do some polynomial expansion, that is allowing some interactions among the original features, with some feature function $\phi(\cdot)$; then,

$$\hat{y} = \sigma\left(\sum_i \alpha_i \left(x_i^T x\right)\right) \Rightarrow \hat{y} = \sigma\left(\sum_i \alpha_i \left(\phi\left(x_i\right)^T \phi\left(x\right)\right)\right)$$

Instead of coming up with some feature function that are good to separate the data points (not so easy), we could try to come up with such inner product.

In other words, whenever we write down a function that is positive definite and symmetric in two vectors $\mathbf{x}_i$ and $\mathbf{x}_j$, there always exists a function $\phi(\cdot)$ so that $k\left(\mathbf{x}_i, \mathbf{x}_j\right)$ is the inner product in the feature space $\phi\left(\mathbf{x}_i\right)^T \phi\left(\mathbf{x}\right)$. More generally, for any kernel $k(\cdot)$:

$$\hat{y} = \sigma \left(\sum_i \alpha_i k\left(\mathbf{x}_i \mathbf{x}\right) \right)$$

This translate, in practice, as follows: if we compute explicit polynomials from our 100-dimensional original dataset, and we perform all the possibile interaction among them, then my new dataset become $(n \cdot 100)^d$, where d is the degree of the polynomial, and n is the number of samples in the orginal data. This is not really feasible, so if we just use the kernel trick, we need to compute the inner product in the training data. For example:

- $x = (1,2,3)$ and $y = (4,5,6)$;

- $\phi(x) = x^2 = (1,2,3,2,4,6,3,6,9)$;

- $\phi(y) = y^2 = (16,20,24,20,25,30,24,30,36)$;

- $\phi\left(\mathbf{x}\right)^T \phi\left(\mathbf{y}\right) = (16 + 40 + 72 + 40 + 100 + 180 + 72 + 180 + 324) = 1024$

If, instead, we use the kernel trick, then $k(x,y) = (x^T y)^2 = (4 + 10 + 18)^2 = 32^2 = 1024$

2.6.2 Practical Classification Example: Face Recognition

It's time to see a useful application of SVM to a very practical, yet crucial, problem in computer vision: face recognition. This example is publicy available in either the repository of the well-written book by Vanderplas (2016) or in the scikit-learn website at the following stable link: https://scikit-learn.org/stable/auto_examples/applications/plot_face_recognition.html. Since it is a very good example, it is worth to be mentioned here as well.

We will use a very famous dataset, called *Labelled Faces in the Wild*, which consists of 1288 faces of famous people, and it is available at http://vis-www.cs.umass.edu/lfw/lfw-funneled.tgz. However, note that it can be easily imported via scikit-learn from the datasets class with the following command:

```
In [44]: from sklearn.datasets import fetch_lfw_people
```

The interested reader should also note that the scikit API provides another faces dataset, called the *Olivetti faces dataset*, which consists of ten different images for each subject, taken with different facial expressions (open / closed eyes, smiling / not smiling) and facial details (glasses / no glasses). This dataset can also be used for a similar applications as the one shown in this Section.

```
In [45]: faces = fetch_lfw_people(min_faces_per_person=60)
```

Each image consists of 1850 features: we could proceed by simply using each of them in the model, but it is more useful to use some sort of preprocessor to extract more meaningful features; here we will use Principal Component Analysis (PCA), which was described in Section 1.4 to extract 150 fundamental components to feed into our Support Vector Machine Classifier. To do so, we jointly use the preprocessor and the classifier into a single pipeline:

```
In [46]:   from sklearn.svm import SVC
           from sklearn.decomposition import PCA
           from sklearn.pipeline import make_pipeline
           from sklearn.model_selection import train_test_split
           pca = PCA(n_components=150, whiten=True, random_state=42,
                            svd_solver='randomized')
           svc = SVC(kernel='rbf', class_weight='balanced')
           model = make_pipeline(pca, svc)
           X_train,X_test,y_train,y_test = train_test_split(faces.data,
               faces.target, test_size=0.3, random_state=42)
```

To get better performances, we can use a grid search cross-validation to explore random combinations of parameters. Here we will adjust C, which controls the margin hardness, and γ, which controls the size of the radial basis function kernel, and determine the best model.

```
In [47]:  from sklearn.model_selection import GridSearchCV
          param_grid = {'svc__C': [1,5,10,50],
                        'svc__gamma': [0.001,0.0005,0.01,0.1]}
          grid = GridSearchCV(model,param_grid=param_grid, cv=10)
          grid.fit(X_train,y_train)
          print(grid.best_params_)
          print(grid.best_score_)

{'svc__C': 5, 'svc__gamma': 0.001}
0.829268292683
```

We now predict on the test set, using the best model we have just spotted. In the next snippet, we also show a bunch of picture taken from the test set, labelled by the target: if their color is red, then the model missclassified the image.

Predicted Names; Incorrect Labels in Red

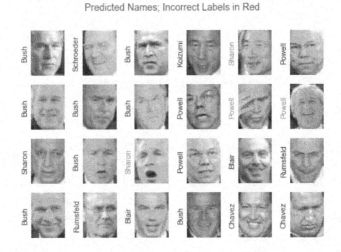

Figure 2.20: Predicted sample names. Incorrect labels are shown in red.

```
In [48]:  model = grid.best_estimator_
          yfit = model.predict(X_test)

In [49]:  fig, ax = plt.subplots(4, 6)
          for i, axi in enumerate(ax.flat):
```

```
axi.imshow(X_test[i].reshape(62, 47), cmap='bone')
axi.set(xticks=[], yticks=[])
axi.set_ylabel(
        faces.target_names[yfit[i]].split()[-1],
        color='black' if yfit[i] == y_test[i]
        else 'red')
fig.suptitle('Predicted Names; Incorrect Labels in Red',size=14)
plt.show()
```

Out of this small sample, our optimal estimator mislabeled only a few single face (Bush's face was mislabeled three times). We can get a better sense of our estimator's performance using the classification report, which lists recovery statistics label by label, as well as we also display the confusion matrix between these labelled classes. This is shown in Figure 2.21, which helps us get a sense of which labels are likely to be confused by the estimator. The performances are pretty good, which shows the SVC is a good estimator for this kind of data.

```
In [50]: labels = list(faces.target_names)
         classification_plots.confusion_matrix(y_test, yfit,
                                    cmap='YlGnBu',
                                    xticklabels=labels,
                                    yticklabels=labels)

In [51]: print(classification_report(y_test,yfit,target_names=labels))
```

	precision	recall	f1-score	support
Ariel Sharon	0.68	0.88	0.77	17
Colin Powell	0.80	0.86	0.83	84
Donald Rumsfeld	0.67	0.89	0.76	36
George W Bush	0.91	0.77	0.83	146
Gerhard Schroeder	0.70	0.75	0.72	28
Hugo Chavez	0.89	0.63	0.74	27
Junichiro Koizumi	0.79	0.94	0.86	16
Tony Blair	0.72	0.76	0.74	51
accuracy			0.80	405
macro avg	0.77	0.81	0.78	405
weighted avg	0.81	0.80	0.80	405

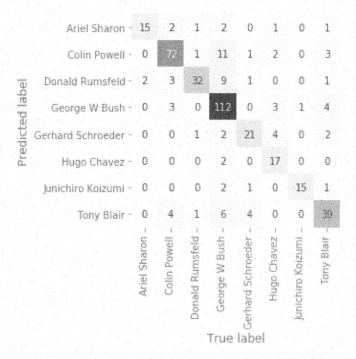

Figure 2.21: Model Performance on the Face Dataset using PCA and SVM together.

Chapter 3

Beyond Linearity: Ensemble Methods for Machine Learning

3.1 Introduction

A popular way to tackle non-linearity in the available data is to use Tree based learning algorithms, which are considered one of the best family of supervised learning methods. Decision Tree algorithms belongs to this family of models, which have gained a remarkable popularity thanks to their predictive power, stability and ease of interpretation. Decision Tree algorithms are referred to as CARTs (Classification and Regression Trees), which is a term proposed by Breiman et al. (1984).

Classification tree analysis is employed when the predicted outcome is the discrete class to which the data example belongs to. Regression tree analysis, instead, is used when the predicted outcome is a continuous variable (e.g. the price of a house, or a patient's length of stay in a hospital). Trees in both regression and classification have many similarities, but they also have many differences, such as the procedure used to determine where to split the tree. More specifically, classification trees split the data based on the concept of purity of the node, and notably we aim at maximizing the decrease of impurity for each split, whereas for regression tasks, we typically fit the model to the set of explanatory variables, giving less attention to those features where their inclusion increase the prediction error for those nodes. In this Chapter, we are going to investigate mainly ensemble and boosting algorithms, trying to highlight pros and cons for each single proposed method.

3.2   Ensemble Methods

CARTs have many advantages: they are easy to understand, and their output is easy to interpret. In addition, CARTs are easy to use and their flexibility gives them an ability to describe non-linear dependencies between features and labels.

Furthermore, compared to a linear model, where preprocessing plays a key role in the dataset creation phase (and therefore in training performance), CARTs do not need a lot of feature preprocessing of the features before feeding them into the model as the training set.

Unfortunately, CARTs have also many limitations: a classification tree, for example, is only able to produce orthogonal decision boundaries. CARTs are also very sensitive to small variations in the training set: notably, when an example is removed from the training set, the estimated parameters may drammatically change (see the book by Zumel and Mount (2014) for further details).

CARTs also suffer from high variance when they are trained without constraints. In such cases, they might overfit the training set. Recall that overfitting describes the situation in which the choosen model describes the training data well, but it does not generalize to unseen data, which is the objective of statistical learning.

A solution that takes advantage of the flexibility of CARTs while reducing their tendency to memorize noise is Ensemble Learning. The key idea is that different models, such as Logistic Regression or a Support Vector Classifier, or even a Decision Tree, are trained on the same dataset, and each model makes its own prediction; a meta-model then aggregates the predictions of individuals models and outputs a final prediction. The result is that the final prediction is more robust and less prone to errors than each individual model.

Let us now take a look of an Ensembling Method called Voting Classifier: the ensemble here consists of M different classifiers making the predictions $P_i \in \{0, 1\}$ for $i = 1, \ldots, M$. The meta-model outputs the final prediction by hard voting, which basically consists in the most frequent output score produced by the ensemble of classifiers.

To show how Voting Classifier works in Python, we use the Heart Disease Dataset, available in the book-specific GitHub repository.

```
In [1]: import pandas as pd
        import numpy as np
        import matplotlib.pyplot as plt
        import seaborn as sns
        from egeaML import DataIngestion, Preprocessing, model_fitting
```

```
from egeaML import xgboost, classification_plots
from sklearn.linear_model import LogisticRegression
from sklearn.tree import DecisionTreeClassifier
from sklearn.svm import SVC
from sklearn.ensemble import VotingClassifier, BaggingClassifier
from sklearn.ensemble import RandomForestClassifier,
from sklearn.ensemble import RandomForestRegressor
from sklearn.model_selection import train_test_split,GridSearchCV
from sklearn.metrics import classification_report, accuracy_score
from sklearn.metrics import mean_squared_error as MSE
```

Using TensorFlow backend.

We use the DataIngestion book-specific class to load the data. Let us load the features and the target separately, and then split the data into train and test set.

```
In [2]: di = DataIngestion(df='heart.csv', col_to_drop= ['Thal'],
                    col_target='AHD')
        X = di.features()
        y = di.target().apply(lambda x: 1 if x=='Yes' else 0)
        X_train, X_test, y_train, y_test = train_test_split(X,y,
                stratify=y, test_size=0.3, random_state=42)
        X_train = X_train.reset_index(drop=True)
        y_train = y_train.reset_index(drop=True)
        X_test = X_test.reset_index(drop=True)
        y_test = y_test.reset_index(drop=True)
        train = pd.concat([X_train,y_train],axis=1)
        test = pd.concat([X_test,y_test],axis=1)
```

We print the first five examples, running the following snippet:

```
In [3]:  pd.set_option('display.max_columns', 100)
         train.head()
```

Out[3]:		Age	Sex	ChestPain	RestBP	Chol	Fbs	RestECG	MaxHR	ExAng	Oldpeak \
	0	52	0	nonanginal	136	196	0	2	169	0	0.1
	1	59	1	nonanginal	150	212	1	0	157	0	1.6
	2	35	1	nontypical	122	192	0	0	174	0	0.0
	3	58	1	asymptomatic	128	259	0	2	130	1	3.0
	4	71	0	nontypical	160	302	0	0	162	0	0.4

```
     Slope   Ca  AHD
0       2  0.0    0
1       1  0.0    0
2       1  0.0    0
3       2  2.0    1
4       1  2.0    0
```

Now, we see there is a categorical column, i.e. ChestPain, which describes the pain suffered by the patient. To train a model, we have to do some preprocessing, which requires to have all numerical columns in our dataframe before ingesting it into the model. We make use of the book-class Preprocessing to perform this fundamental step.

```
In [4]:  cat_cols = ['ChestPain']
         df_train= Preprocessing(columns = cat_cols,X=train).dummization()
         df_test = Preprocessing(columns = cat_cols,X=test).dummization()
         X_train_clean = df_train.drop(['AHD'],axis=1)
         y_train_clean = df_train['AHD']
         X_test_clean = df_test.drop(['AHD'],axis=1)
         y_test_clean = df_test['AHD']

In [5]:  X_train_clean.head()
```

```
Out[5]:     Age  Sex  RestBP  Chol  Fbs  RestECG  MaxHR  ExAng  Oldpeak  Slope \
        0    52    0     136   196    0        2    169      0      0.1      2
        1    59    1     150   212    1        0    157      0      1.6      1
        2    35    1     122   192    0        0    174      0      0.0      1
        3    58    1     128   259    0        2    130      1      3.0      2
        4    71    0     160   302    0        0    162      0      0.4      1
```

```
            Ca     ChestPain_asymptomatic  ChestPain_nonanginal  \
        0   0.0                         0                     1
        1   0.0                         0                     1
        2   0.0                         0                     0
        3   2.0                         1                     0
        4   2.0                         0                     0
```

```
            ChestPain_nontypical  ChestPain_typical
        0                      0                  0
        1                      0                  0
        2                      1                  0
        3                      0                  0
        4                      1                  0
```

We now fit a series of independent models, and see which one better performs with the given data. In particular, we are going to fit a

- Logistic Regression Model;

- Decicion Tree Classifier;

- Support Vector Classifier

and investigate the individual performances on the test set. We will make use of the book-class model_fitting, which is available in the egeaML library. We specify the models before calling the method fitting_models() of the class model_fitting, and then the user is asked again to specify the names of the models, so that the machine is going to fit the data to the desired models, and test their accuracy on unseen data. As an exercise, one could extend it to a different set of models, as well as generalizing it as a dynamic method for fitting ML models, but that task is beyond the scope of this book.

```
In [6]: lr = LogisticRegression()
        dt = DecisionTreeClassifier()
        svc = SVC()

In [7]: fitting = model_fitting(n=3)
        models_dict = fitting.models_def(
                    model_one ='Logistic Regression', abb1='lr',
                    model_two = 'Decision Tree Clf', abb2 = 'dt',
                    model_three = 'Support Vector Clf', abb3='svc')
        models_dict

Out[7]: {'Logistic Regression': 'lr',
         'Decision Tree Clf': 'dt',
         'Support Vector Clf': 'svc'}

In [8]: models_ = model_fitting(n=3).get_models(
                    models_dict=models_dict,
                        model_one='LogisticRegression',
                        model_two='DecisionTreeClassifier',
                        model_three='SVC' )

In [9]: model_fitting(n=3).fitting_models(models= models_,
                        X_train=X_train_clean,
```

```
                                 y_train=y_train_clean,
                                 X_test=X_test_clean,
                                 y_test=y_test_clean)
```

```
Logistic Regression : 0.8242
Decision Tree Clf : 0.7582
Support Vector Clf : 0.5275
```

It looks like the Logistic Regression model is the one which performs the best with the given data. As usual, this might be given by chance, so we could think of using the Voting Classifier we have discussed to obtain a score that takes into account all the fitted models.

```
In [10]:  clfs = [('Logistic Regression', lr),
                   ('Decision Tree', dt),
                   ('Support Vector Classifier', svc)
                  ]
          vc = VotingClassifier(estimators=clfs)
          vc.fit(X_train_clean,y_train_clean)
          y_pred = vc.predict(X_test_clean)
          score = format(accuracy_score(y_test_clean,y_pred), '.4f')
          print("Voting Classifier : {}".format(score))
```

```
Voting Classifier : 0.8132
```

Not surprisingly, the Voting Classifier performs as good as the Logistic Regression and performs better than the Decision Tree, outperforming the Support Vector Classifier.

3.2.1   Boostrap Aggregation

We now introduce a family of models that goes under the name of Boostrap Aggregation, also known as Bagging, which is a way to reduce training variance, and to avoid overfitting.

The Voting Classifier is an ensemble of models that are fit to the same training set using different algorithms, and that a test example is feedeed into each model, but the final prediction is obtained by majority voting.

In Boostrap Aggregation, instead, the ensemble is formed by models that share the same baseline algorithm, but differently from the Voting Classifier, where each model is trained on the whole training set, here each model is trained on a different subset of the data, yet keeping all the features.

The ideal scenario to reduce the variance - and to increase the prediction accuracy - is to take many different training sets from the available dataset, build a separate model for each of them, and averaging the resulting predictions. Notably, however, we do not have access to multiple training sets, and therefore we typically resort to boostrap. Bostrapping means taking repeated random samples with replacement from the training dataset: this allows one to fit a model on a series of training sets that share a common base.

For a given test example, we record the class predicted by each of the model and the overall prediction is the most commonly occurring class among these predictions. According to the problem we are facing on, the final prediction is going to be produced accordingly. On the one hand, when dealing with classifications, the final prediction is obtained by majority voting. On the other hand, the final prediction is the average of the predictions made by the individual models, forming the ensemble when we focus on Regression analysis.

We firstly fit a Decision Tree Classifier without specifying parameters.

```
In [11]:   dt = DecisionTreeClassifier()
           dt.fit(X_train_clean,y_train_clean)
           y_pred_bc = dt.predict(X_test_clean)
           score = accuracy_score(y_test_clean,y_pred_bc)
           print('Test Accuracy of: ' + str(score))
```

Test Accuracy of: 0.7582417582417582

Note that if you run the above code in your console, you might obtain a different result: this is because bagging is based on random boostrap of the training set. Since hyperparameters are not learned from the data, but must be tuned, we perform a GridSearch on two hyperparameters of the Decision Tree, that is max_depth, and min_samples_leaf, which describes the maximum depth of the tree and the minimum percentage of samples per leaf, respectively. In this way, we are going to search for the set of optimal hyperparameters that identifies the optimal learning algorithm and that allows to obtain the best model performances.

```
In [12]:   grid = {'max_depth':[3,4,5,6],
                   'min_samples_leaf':[0.5,1,3,5,8,10]}
           dt_ = GridSearchCV(dt, grid, scoring='accuracy',
                   cv=5,n_jobs=-1, verbose=0)
```

```
dt_.fit(X_train_clean,y_train_clean)
y_pred_bc = dt_.predict(X_test_clean)
score = accuracy_score(y_test_clean,y_pred_bc)
print('Test Accuracy of: ' + str(score))
print('Best params: {}'.format(dt_.best_params_))
```

```
Test Accuracy of: 0.7802197802197802
Best params: {'max_depth': 4, 'min_samples_leaf': 5}
```

Note that setting n_jobs equal to -1 has the effect that all the available cpu cores are used in the computation phase. If we implement Bagging technique on the data, we see that it slightly performs better than the base estimator dt we have defined before, that is the Decision Tree Classifier.

```
In [13]:   dt = DecisionTreeClassifier(max_depth=4, min_samples_leaf=5)
           bc = BaggingClassifier(base_estimator =dt_, n_estimators=300,
                                                  n_jobs=-1)
           bc.fit(X_train_clean,y_train_clean)
           y_pred_bc = bc.predict(X_test_clean)
           score = accuracy_score(y_test_clean,y_pred_bc)
           print('Test Accuracy of: ' + str(score))
```

```
Test Accuracy of: 0.7912087912087912
```

3.2.2   Out-of-Bag Estimation

Recall that in Bagging, some instances might be sampled several times for one model. On the other hand, other instances may not be sampled at all. On average, for each model, 67% of the training examples are sampled the remaining 33% constitute what is known as the OOB instances: these can be used to estimate the performance of the ensemble without the need for cross-validation, and hence reducing the efforts in obtaining the best model.

To do that, we will fit a BaggingClassifier by specifying the argument oob_score as True: this allows to evaluate the OOB-accuracy of the Bagging Classifier after the fit on the training.

```
In [14]: dt = DecisionTreeClassifier(max_depth=4, min_samples_leaf=5)
         bc = BaggingClassifier(base_estimator =dt_, n_estimators=300,
```

```
                              oob_score=True, n_jobs=-1)
    bc.fit(X_train_clean,y_train_clean)
    y_pred_bc = bc.predict(X_test_clean)
    score = accuracy_score(y_test_clean,y_pred_bc)
    oob_score = bc.oob_score_
    print('Test Accuracy of: ' + str(score))
    print('OOB: ' + str(oob_score))
```

```
Test Accuracy of: 0.7912087912087912
OOB: 0.8066037735849056
```

They are slightly different: this clearly shows how OOB-evaluation can be an efficient technique to obtain the performance estimate of a bagged-ensemble on unseen
data without performing cross-validation.

3.3 Random Forests

Random Forests is an ensemble method that uses a Decision Tree as a base estimator.
It was proposed by Breiman in 2001, and since then, he has been extremely used
by researchers and practitioners. At the time this book was written, that paper had
more than 26,000 citations.

In Random Forests, each estimator is trained on a different boostrap sample having the same size as the training set. This model introduces further randomization
than Bagging when training each of the base estimators. Let p be the total number
of available features in the training dataset. In classification problems, when each
tree is trained, only $\sqrt{p}$ features are used at each node without replacement. For Regression, instead, only $\frac{p}{3}$ features are used at each node. The node is then split using
the sampled feature (among the choosen ones) that maximizes information gain. To
make a new prediction on a new point, then we take the majority vote (in case of
classification) or we average the scoring results (in case of regression).

3.3.1 Random Forests Classifier

```
In [15]:   rf = RandomForestClassifier(n_estimators=30)
           rf.fit(X_train_clean,y_train_clean)
           y_pred = rf.predict(X_test_clean)
           print(classification_report(y_pred, y_test_clean))
```

	precision	recall	f1-score	support
0	0.90	0.80	0.85	55
1	0.74	0.86	0.79	36
accuracy			0.82	91
macro avg	0.82	0.83	0.82	91
weighted avg	0.83	0.82	0.83	91

Feature Importance

When a random forest is trained, we can easily access to the global feature importance attribute, which describe the ability of each feature to reduce impurity at each
node. This is expressed as the weight of that particular feature in training and prediction, expressed in percentage.

To visualize it, we create a sorted pandas series of the feature importances, which is
then plotted. Note that here we are just returning the first top ten features, and each
of them is shown horizontally. This is shown in Figure 3.1.

```
In [16]: importance_rf = pd.Series(rf.feature_importances_,
                                    index=X_train_clean.columns)
         importance_rf_sorted = importance_rf.sort_values()
         importance_rf_sorted.nlargest(20).plot(kind='barh', color='orange')
         plt.title("Feature Importance Random Forest")
         plt.show()
```

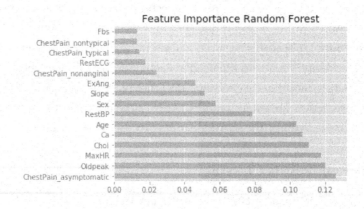

Figure 3.1: Feature (global) importance obtained by fitting a random Forest Classifier
on the Heart Disease Dataset.

The following snippet code shows the role of pruning in controlling overfitting, that is it shows how accuracy varies as max_depth varies. As shown in Figure 3.2, it seems after n_estimators= 5 we tend to overfit.

```
In [17]: max_depth = range(1,20)
         train_scores = []
         test_scores = []
         for a in max_depth:
             tree = RandomForestClassifier(random_state=0,max_depth=a)
             tree.fit(X_train_clean,y_train_clean)
             train_scores.append(tree.score(X_train_clean,y_train_clean))
             test_scores.append(tree.score(X_test_clean,y_test_clean))

In [18]: plt.plot(max_depth, test_scores, train_scores)
         plt.xlabel('max_depth')
         plt.ylabel('Random Forest Accuracy')
         plt.show()
```

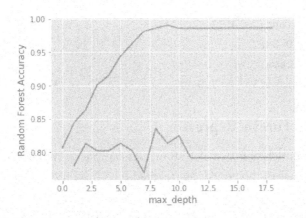

Figure 3.2: The role of pruning in control overfitting.

We have therefore seen many different models applied on this dataset. It seems that Random Forests is the ensemble method that shows the best performances. However, Logistic regression is still the model that outperforms the rest, which is reasonable when we have a small dataset with some linear relationship among some features.

To see this, we implement the following function, which outputs the score of the models we have investigated so far in this section:

```
In [19]:  def fitting_models():
              lr=LogisticRegression()
              dt = DecisionTreeClassifier()
              svc = SVC()
              rfc = RandomForestClassifier()
              clfs = [('Logistic Regression', lr),
                      ('Decision Tree', dt),
                      ('Support Vector Classifier', svc),
                      ('Random Forest Classifier', rfc)
                     ]


              for name,clf in clfs:
                  clf.fit(X_train,y_train)
                  pred = clf.predict(X_test)
                  score = format(accuracy_score(y_test,pred), '.4f')
                  print("{} : {}".format(name,score))


          fitting_models()

Logistic Regression : 0.9533
Decision Tree : 0.8422
Support Vector Classifier : 0.4867
Random Forest Classifier : 0.9467
```

3.3.2   Random Forests Regressor

For the sake of completeness, we also show an example of Regression Random Forest. We will make use of the hourly-aggregated data from the Washington D.C. Bike Sharing system, publicy available at https://www.capitalbikeshare.com/system-data. This dataset was used by Fanaee and Gama (2013) in their nice, well-written paper.

```
In [20]: di = DataIngestion(df='bike_sharing.csv', col_to_drop=None,
                                                   col_target='cnt')
         X_rf = di.features()
         y_rf = di.target()

In [21]:  X_train, X_test, y_train, y_test = train_test_split(X_rf,
                     y_rf,test_size=0.3, random_state=42)
```

```
            X_train = X_train.reset_index(drop=True)
            y_train = y_train.reset_index(drop=True)
            X_test = X_test.reset_index(drop=True)
            y_test = y_test.reset_index(drop=True)

In [22]:    rf = RandomForestRegressor(n_estimators=30)
            rf.fit(X_train,y_train)
            y_pred = rf.predict(X_test)

In [23]:    rmse_test = MSE(y_test,y_pred)**(1/2)
            print('RMSE of RF (Test Set): {:.4f}'.format(rmse_test))

RMSE of RF (Test Set): 60.3499
```

Note that in order to obtain a more robust result, the reader is invited to perform a grid search cross-validation, since the one just obtained might suffer from the way the data were splitted.

3.4 Boosting Methods

Boosting refers to a family of ensemble methods in which many predictors are trained sequentially, and each predictor learns from the errors of its predecessor. In particular, the idea is that new trees are created to reduce the residual errors in the predictions from the existing sequence of trees. More formally, in boosting many weak learners are combined to form a strong learner. A weak learner is a model that performs slightly better than random guessing. We will investigate three Boosting algorithm: the AdaBoost, the Gradient Boosting, the XGBoost and finally the CatBoost.

3.4.1 AdaBoost

This algorithm was introduced by Freund and Schapire (1997). In AdaBoost each predictor pays more attention to the instances wrongly predicted by its predecessor, by constantly changing the weights of training instances. Furthermore, each predictor is assigned a coefficient α that weights its contribution in the ensemble's final prediction.

Note that α depends on the predictor's training error: basically, we fit the first model on the inital dataset, and the training error for model one is determined. This error can then be used to determine α_1, which is predictor one coefficient.

α_1 is then used to determine the weights α_2 of the training instances for model two: here, the incorrectly predicted examples acquire higher weights, and are used to train model two. In this case, the predictor is forced to pay more attention to the incorrectly predicted examples. This process is repeated sequentially, until the N predictors forming the ensemble are trained. An important parameter used in training is the learning rate $\eta \in (0,1)$: the learning rate, also called shrinkage, is used to prevent overfitting since it reduces the influence of each individual learner and leaves space for future ones to improve the overall ensemble. Unfortunately, there is a trade-off between learning_rate and the number of trained trees. A smaller value of the learning rate should be compensated by a greater number of estimators. Once all the predictors in the ensemble are trained, the label of a new example can be predicted depending on the nature of the problem. For classification, each predictor predicts the label of a new instance, and the ensemble prediction is obtained by weighted majority voting. For regression, the same procedure applies and the ensemble's prediction is obtained by performing a weighted average.

```
In [24]: from sklearn.ensemble import AdaBoostClassifier
         from sklearn.metrics import roc_auc_score
         dt = DecisionTreeClassifier(max_depth=1)
         ada_clf = AdaBoostClassifier(base_estimator=dt,n_estimators=100)
         ada_clf.fit(X_train_clean, y_train_clean)
         y_pred_proba = ada_clf.predict_proba(X_test_clean)[:,1]
         ada_clf_roc_auc = roc_auc_score(y_test_clean, y_pred_proba)
         print(format(ada_clf_roc_auc, '.4f'))
```

0.8523

3.4.2   Gradient Boosting

The Gradient Boosting is another very popular ensemble method, proposed by Friedman (2001) that combines multiple decision trees to create a more robust model. Indeed, in contrast to AdaBoost, the weights of the training examples are not adjusted but each predictor is trained using the residual errors of its predecessor as labels. Although gradient boosted trees are very popular within the ML community, we should note that gradient boosted trees notably uses extremely shallow trees, say of depth ranging from one to five, which makes the model smaller in terms of memory and makes predictions fasters. Those shallow trees play the role of weak learners, and the performance is improved by adding more and more shallow trees to the predictor. Practically, there are (at least) three important parameters that one should take care of when tuning a gradient boosted tree:

1. Number of Trees in the ensemble (n_estimators), which controls the model complexity;

2. Learning Rate (learning_rate), which controls how strongly each tree tries to correct the mistakes of the previous trees;

3. Pre-pruning (max_depth), which controls the number of levels for each tree.

Note that a higher learning rate translates into a more complex model, since under this scenario each tree can make stronger corrections on the training set.

In scikit-learn, the class GradientBoostingClassifier is used to easily fit a gradient boosting classifier.

```
In [25]: from sklearn.ensemble import GradientBoostingClassifier
         gbc = GradientBoostingClassifier(n_estimators=40)
         gbc.fit(X_train_clean, y_train_clean)
         gbc.score(X_test_clean, y_test_clean)
```

```
Out[25]: 0.8131868131868132
```

We can cross-validate the result, as we have done previously with other ensemble techniques, as follows:

```
In [26]: n_estimators = [30,50,80] # Number of trees
         max_depth = [1,3,5] # Maximum n of levels in each tree
         learning_rate = [0.001, 0.01, 0.1] # model complexity
         param_grid_ = {'n_estimators': n_estimators,
                        'max_depth': max_depth,
                        'learning_rate': learning_rate
                       }
```

```
In [27]: grid = GridSearchCV(gbc,param_grid=param_grid_, cv=5)
         grid.fit(X_train_clean,y_train_clean)
         print(grid.best_params_)
         print(grid.best_score_)
         yfit_gbc = grid.predict(X_test_clean)
```

```
{'learning_rate': 0.1, 'max_depth': 1, 'n_estimators': 30}
0.7971698113207547
```

```
In [28]: print(classification_report(y_test_clean,yfit_gbc))
```

	precision	recall	f1-score	support
0	0.76	0.86	0.81	49
1	0.81	0.69	0.74	42
accuracy			0.78	91
macro avg	0.78	0.77	0.78	91
weighted avg	0.78	0.78	0.78	91

Feature selection is also allowed with Boosting algorithm, as shown in Figure 3.3:

```
In [29]: importance_gb = pd.Series(gbc.feature_importances_,
                        index=X_train_clean.columns)
        importance_gb_sorted = importance_gb.sort_values()
        importance_gb_sorted.nlargest(20).plot(kind='barh',
                        color='orange')
        plt.title("Feature Importance Gradient Boosting")
        plt.show()
```

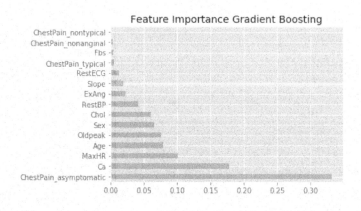

Figure 3.3: Feature global importance in Gradient Boosting Classifier.

Note that differently from Random Forest, the feature importance is notably changed in magnitude: this is one of the main effect of combining many weak learners into a single powerful model. Note also that some features were completely ignored to the Gradient Boosting, or little importance was given to them: this contrasts with the results coming from the Random Forest, where those features were remarkably important.

Practical Tip. If you don't know which model is the best to apply, go with Random Forest: it works quite robustly on any kind of data, but it might be slower than Gradient Boosting, especially on large-scale problems.

3.4.3 Extreme Gradient Boosting (XGBoost)

XGBoost was proposed by the student Chen and his former advisor Guestrin in 2016, and it was originally developed as a C++ command-line application. Fastly enough, it was adopted by the Machine learning community since it outperforms many algorithms, and it has been shown to achieve state-of-the-art performances on a variety of benchmark machine learning datasets. As expected, the model start immediately appearing in many other languages, such as Python, Julia, and Scala. One of the principal reasons XGBoost became so popular is in its speed and performances. However, because the core of XGBoost algorithm is parallelizable, it can deal with all of the processing power of modern multicore computers. Furthermore, it is parallelizable onto GPU's and across networks of computers, making it feasible to train models on very large datasets on the order of hundreds of millions of training examples. We import the xgboost library in order to fit a model.

```
In [30]: import xgboost as xgb
```

Note that XGBoost should be considered, in principle, for any supervised problem that satisfies the following criteria:

- the dataset under investigation is characterized by having a set of examples significantly large than the number of features;

- there are possible outliers in the input space;

- you have a mixture of categorical and continuous variables;

- in Classification tasks, the target is unbalanced

Note also that XGBoost is consistent to missing values, which means that we do not need to impute any value before fitting (see Section 3.4 of the seminal paper by Chen and Guestrin for further details on this issue). Furthermore, while in Random Forests we typically subsample the features in each node, with XGBoost we subsample the features for the whole tree: this not only permits to build trees faster but also it prevents overfitting.

More technically, XGBoost is based on the principle of weak-learner, where each predictor could be improved by sequentially training new trees to the model. This litterally means that the residual errors in the predictions are dynamically correct. We completely follow the notation in Chen and Guestrin (2016), so please refer to that article for further details. Let us consider a set of training examples (x_i, y_i), $i = 1, \ldots, n$ and $x \in \mathbb{R}^k$. Suppose that to predict the output, a classical tree ensemble algorithm is used, where K additive functions f_k in the space of CARTs are trained. The predicted output is given by the sum of each individual function prediction,

$$\hat{y} = \sum_k f_k(x_i)$$

To learn the set of functions used in the model, at step t we minimize the following regularized objective function (obtained with a Taylor approximation of second order)

$$\mathcal{L}^{(t)} \simeq \sum_{i=1}^n l\left(\left(y_i, \hat{y}^{(t-1)}\right) + g_i\, f_t(x_i) + \frac{1}{2}h_i f_t^2(x_i) \right) + \Omega(f_t)$$

where:

- $\mathcal{L}(\hat{y}, y) = -\left(y \log(\hat{y}) + (1 - y)\,()\right)$ is a differentiable convex loss function that computes the prediction error for each single training example;

- $g_i = \partial_{\hat{y}^{(t-1)}} l\left(y_i, \hat{y}^{(t-1)}\right)$ and $h_i = \partial_{\hat{y}^{(t-1)}}^2 l\left(y_i, \hat{y}^{(t-1)}\right)$ are the first and second order gradient statistics on the loss function;

- $\Omega(f) = \gamma |f(x)| + \frac{1}{2}\lambda ||\omega||^2$, with $|f(x)|$ defines the number of leafs of tree, and ω is the weight vector containing each leaf score.

Another very interesting feature related to XGBoost is that it incorporates a penalization that can be understood as a mixture between a $\mathcal{L}_1$ (on the parameter γ) and $\mathcal{L}_2$ (on the parameter λ) penalty, which practically translates into (global) feature importance and selection. We have already seen how importance is computed in Random Forest, and the same arguments apply here with boosted decision trees: for each feature, it returns a score that indicates how important that feature was in the construction of the new added trees within the model, which then allow attributes to be ranked and compared to each other. Importance is calculated for a single decision tree by the amount that each attribute split point improves the performance measure, weighted by the number of observations the node is responsible for. The performance measure may be the Gini index used to select the split points in Classifications or the variance in Regression trees. The feature importances are then averaged across all of the the decision trees within the model. Although this is widely used in practice, global feature selection has a drawback: it does not explain each prediction score locally. In other words, it does not allow to explain to a non-technical audience which features have contributed the most in the construction of each single score: this is however explained by the SHAP (SHapley Additive exPlanations), proposed by Lundeber and Lee (2017), which is a unified approach to explain the output of any machine learning model. The idea behind Shapley values comes from a seminal paper by Shapley (1953) related to Game Theory, and tells in which measure the value of the feature X influence the prediction a particular example, compared to the average prediction for the dataset, which is the baseline of the model. Hence, the marginal contribution would mean how much each feature forces the prediction to move away from that baseline. The SHAP is model agnostic, so in principle, can be applied to any model. As an illustrative example, we take the example proposed by Lundeberg in his GitHub repository https://github.com/slundberg/shap: this small example fit an XGBoost regressor on the Boston House Dataset.

```
In [31]:  import shap
          X_boston,y_boston = shap.datasets.boston()
          model_ = xgb.train({"learning_rate": 0.01},
          xgb.DMatrix(X_boston, label=y_boston), 100)

          explainer = shap.TreeExplainer(model_)
          shap_values = explainer.shap_values(X_boston)

          shap.force_plot(explainer.expected_value, shap_values[3,:],
            X_boston.iloc[3,:],matplotlib=True)
```

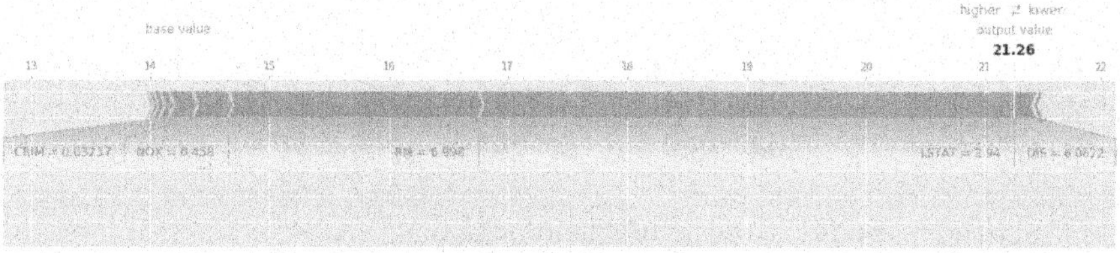

Figure 3.4: Raw SHAP Score for the fourth observation, with the (negative and positive) effect of some features explained. Note that in red we have features that move positively away from the baseline, whereas in blue the ones which affect negatively this pattern.

Remark. To overcome overfitting, XGBoost applies a shrinkage factor (also called learning rate) that controls the weighting of new trees added to the model. In particular, setting values less than 0.1 typically has the effect of making less corrections for each tree added to the model. This in turn results in more trees that must be added to the model. Note also that typically the performance is positively correlated with the number of estimators/trees for learning rate smaller than 0.1, but it gets worst for greater learning rate, suggesting that a smaller number of trees may be required to achieve good performances.

XGBoost in Practice: Application to the Heart Dataset

To show how XGBoost works in practice, we still use the Heart dataset; in particular, we use XGBoost to predict the probability of having a heart attack given a set of features. To fit the model, we use the fitting method from the book-specific xgboost Class. This function basically search for the best hyperparameters values via cross-validation, and then fit the best XGBoost Classifier model on the training data. Note that we mst specify the parameter grid.

```
In [32]: param_grid = [{'max_depth': np.arange(4, 9, 1),
                        'learning_rate': [0.01,0.05,0.1,0.5,1],
                        'n_estimators': np.arange(100, 601, 100)}]
```

Here I will run the grid search on 150 different combinations of parameters over five different folds: this will take quite a lot, so I suggest you to change the settings if you want to run this function locally on your machine.

```
In [33]: model = xgboost.fitting(X_train_clean, y_train_clean,
                        param_grid = param_grid,
                        n_jobs=-1,cv=5)
```

```
Fitting 5 folds for each of 150 candidates, totalling 750 fits
```

```
[Parallel(n_jobs=1)]: Using backend SequentialBackend ... workers.
[Parallel(n_jobs=1)]: Done 750 out of 750 | elapsed:  3.9min finished
```

```
In [34]: y_pred = model.predict(X_test_clean)
         y_pred_prob = model.best_estimator_.predict_proba(
                        X_test_clean)[:, 1]
```

```
In [35]: print(classification_report(y_test_clean,y_pred))
```

	precision	recall	f1-score	support
0	0.80	0.90	0.85	49
1	0.86	0.74	0.79	42
accuracy			0.82	91
macro avg	0.83	0.82	0.82	91
weighted avg	0.83	0.82	0.82	91

The performances are pretty good but we are not outperforming the Random Forests
(on the same set of data). To get a better understanding of our prediction, we make
use of the SHAP values: the following snippet converts the model features into local
scores, stored into a pandas DataFrame, where each column now contains the local
shap value corresponding to that feature.

```
In [36]:  explainer = shap.TreeExplainer(model.best_estimator_)
          shap_values = explainer.shap_values(X_train_clean)
          df_shap_values = pd.DataFrame(shap_values,
                              columns=list(X_train_clean.columns))
```

The next code produces, as output, a plot that shows which features force the model
output away from the base (average model) value. Features increasing the prediction
score are shown in red, whereas those decreasing the prediction score are in blue.

```
In [37]:  shap.initjs()
          shap.force_plot(explainer.expected_value, shap_values[27,:],
                              X_train_clean.iloc[5,:], link='logit')
```

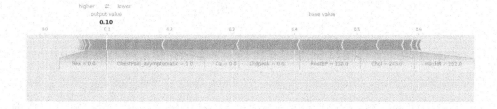

We clearly see that for this particuar example, a score of 0.1 was obtained, and the
top features importance are reported. For instance, being male increases the probability of having a heart disease, whereas either Cholesterol level equal to 243 or an

observed asymptomatic chest pain reduces the aforementioned probability. To complete the picture, let us investigate an example which has been classified as prone to hearth failure:

```
In [38]: shap.force_plot(explainer.expected_value, shap_values[42,:],
                   X_train_clean.iloc[5,:], link='logit')
```

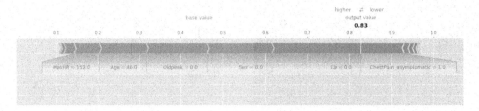

As one might expect, being male, aged 46 with maximum heart rate of 152 significantly increases the score.

Bar chart of mean importance   The following snippet takes the average of the SHAP value magnitudes across the dataset, and plots it as a simple bar chart. The result is shown in Figure 3.5.

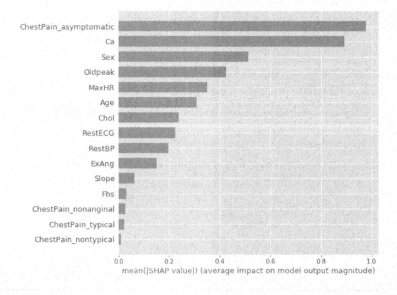

Figure 3.5: Feature global importance as the average of the SHAP value magnitudes across the dataset.

```
In [39]: shap.summary_plot(shap_values, X_train_clean, plot_type="bar")
```

SHAP Summary Plot   To identify the impact of each feature on the model output in the training set, we use a density scatter plot of SHAP values for each feature. Features are sorted by the sum of the SHAP value magnitudes across all samples. The color represents the feature value (red high, blue low). This reveals for example that a high value of the *MaxHR* feature (which describes the maximum Hearth Rate per minute) tends to have a positive impact on the output score than the *Age* feature, but for those samples where *Age* matters it has more impact than *Chol*, which effects tend to be smaller (more compacted towards zero) than the *Age*, which seems to be more spreaded. The result is shown in Figure 3.6.

```
In [40]: shap.summary_plot(shap_values, X_train_clean)
```

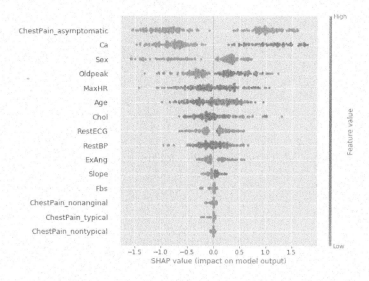

Figure 3.6: Feature Importance for all the dataset units.

SHAP dependence plot   To understand how a single feature affects the output of the model, we can plot the SHAP value of that feature versus the value of the feature for all the examples in a dataset. A SHAP dependence plot showa the effect of a single feature across the whole dataset. SHAP dependence plots are similar to partial dependence plots, but account for the interaction effects present in the features. The vertical dispersion of SHAP values at a single feature value is driven by interaction effects, and another feature is chosen for coloring to highlight possible interactions. Since SHAP values represent a feature's responsibility for a change in the model output, the plot below represents the change in predicted output model as *MaxHR* changes. To help revealing these interactions, dependence_plot automatically selects another feature for coloring. In this case coloring by *Ca* highlights that the average *MaxHR* has higher impact on the positive class for examples with a high *Ca* value. This is shown in Figure 3.7.

In [41]: shap.dependence_plot("MaxHR", shap_values, X_train_clean)

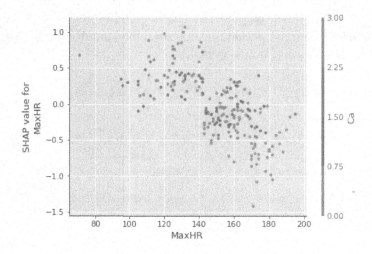

Figure 3.7: Dependence Plot for the feature *MaxHR*.

3.4.4   CatBoost

CatBoost is a new gradient boosting based algorithm, which was introduced by Prokhorenkova et al. (2018), and its performances have been shown to be extremely interesting, compared to other boosting algorithm, such as XGBoost, as reported here:

https://github.com/catboost/benchmarks/tree/master/quality_benchmarks.

In particular, two major advances were introduced in CatBoost: on the one hand, a new boosting schema, called *ordered boosting*, was proposed: differently from classical boosting algorithm, CatBoost divides a given dataset into random permutations, and apply ordered boosting on those random permutations. On the other hand, it smartly deals with categorical features, using a new algorithm for processing categorical features, by building new numerical features based on categorical features and their combinations.

CatBoost actually divides a given dataset into random permutations. By default CatBoost creates four random permutations. With this randomness we can further stop overfitting our model. We can further control this randomness by tuning parameter bagging_temperature.

Note that the ordered boosting typically gets slower with small datasets (i.e. less than 50,000 examples), but it generally has very fast inference, because the algorithm uses specific kind of trees, called *symmetric trees*.

As noted by one of the author, catboost outperforms other available methods on GPU, but that is not true on CPU: typically, the training time on CPU is slower than XGBoost, but this depends on the dataset properties, especially if we are dealing with a very sparse datsaset - catboost does not perform well on those kind of dataset.

Let's see in practice how this algorithm works. We start by importing the usual libraries, plus the catboost library, which comes with the book-specific library egeaML.

```
In [42]: from catboost import CatBoostClassifier, Pool, cv
```

To illustrate this algorithm, we use the Titanic dataset, which contains as target variable the survival classification (that is 1 as alive, 0 as dead). This can be easily imported from the catboost class datasets:

```
In [43]: from catboost.datasets import titanic
         titanic_train, titanic_test = titanic()
         titanic_train.head()
```

```
Out[43]:    PassengerId  Survived  Pclass  \
       0            1         0       3
       1            2         1       1
       2            3         1       3
       3            4         1       1
       4            5         0       3
```

```
                                                  Name     Sex   Age  \
0                           Braund, Mr. Owen Harris    male  22.0
1     Cumings, Mrs. John Bradley (Florence Briggs Th...  female  38.0
2                            Heikkinen, Miss. Laina  female  26.0
3        Futrelle, Mrs. Jacques Heath (Lily May Peel)  female  35.0
4                          Allen, Mr. William Henry    male  35.0
```

```
   SibSp  Parch            Ticket     Fare Cabin Embarked
0      1      0         A/5 21171   7.2500   NaN        S
1      1      0          PC 17599  71.2833   C85        C
2      0      0  STON/02. 3101282   7.9250   NaN        S
```

3	1	0	113803	53.1000	C123	S
4	0	0	373450	8.0500	NaN	S

Before going into the catboost pipeline, let us perform a simple EDA on the Titanic dataset, just to understand the type of the features.

```
In [44]: titanic_train.hist(bins='auto', figsize=(18,22), layout=(5,2))
```

It is clear that some of them are clearly categorical, such as Age, Pclass and SibSp, as shown in Figure 3.8.

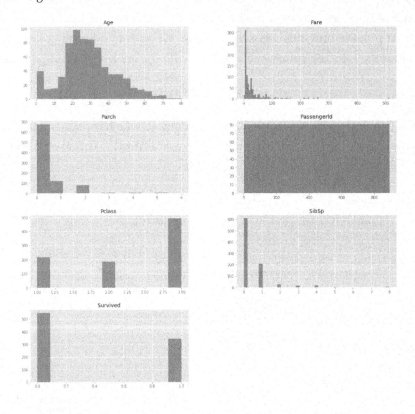

Figure 3.8: Exploratory Data Analysis on the Titanic Dataset.

```
In [45]: titanic_train['Embarked'] = titanic_train['Embarked'].fillna('S')
         titanic_train['Cabin'] = titanic_train['Cabin'].fillna('Undefined')

In [46]: y = titanic_train.Survived
         X = titanic_train.drop(['Survived'],axis=1)
         categorical_features_indices = ['Name', 'Sex', 'Ticket',
                                         'Cabin', 'Embarked', 'SibSp']
```

```
In [47]: X_train, X_test, y_train, y_test = train_test_split(X,y,
                      test_size=0.2,random_state=42)
```

Before fitting the model, it is best practice to do a sort of preprocessing on the data. To do so, we use the class Pool from the catboost library. However, one should note that if most of the features are numerical, and this information is known, it is advisable to preprocess it using the FeaturesData class. See the documentation avilable online at https://catboost.ai/docs/concepts/python-features-data__desc.html. However, if there is no confidence on which features should be considered as numerical, pass the input dataset and the target directly to the Pool class.

```
In [48]: train_pool = Pool(X_train, y_train,
                      cat_features=categorical_features_indices)
```

We are ready to fit the catboost Classifier using the class CatBoostClassifier:

```
In [49]: model = CatBoostClassifier(
             learning_rate=0.01,
             depth=5,
             iterations=300,
             random_seed=42,
             logging_level='Silent',
             allow_writing_files=False
         )

         model.fit(X_train, y_train,
             cat_features=categorical_features_indices)
         model.score(X_train, y_train)
```

```
Out[49]: 0.9115168539325843
```

We got a score of 0.91 in the training set, which is extremely good as first temptative. Note that one could validate this solution using cross-validation, which can be easily implemented using the scikit-learn class or, more easily, the catboost specific class cv. In the next snippet, we extract the global feature importance obtained from this algorithm. The interest reader should also note that the local features importance expressed in terms of Shap Values are available in this framework, though in this particular example are not shown. Figure 3.9 shows the global feature importance on the training set.

```
In [50]: feature_importances = model.get_feature_importance(train_pool)
         feature_names = X_train.columns
         for score, name in sorted(zip(feature_importances,
                     feature_names), reverse=True):
             print('{}: {}'.format(name, score))
```

```
Sex: 43.999999919835176
Pclass: 15.791071087673961
Cabin: 9.100205052848635
Ticket: 7.768885373753501
Embarked: 4.954292045080043
SibSp: 4.930285107310114
Fare: 4.023103732234545
Age: 3.827159943747061
PassengerId: 3.208750197467027
Parch: 2.396247540049968
Name: 0.0
```

```
In [51]: feature_importance_df = pd.DataFrame(sorted(zip(
                 feature_importances, feature_names), reverse=True),
                 columns=['importance','feature'])
         feature_importance_df[['feature','importance']].set_index(
         'feature').plot(kind='barh', figsize=(18, 10),
         fontsize=14)
```

```
Out[51]: <matplotlib.axes._subplots.AxesSubplot at 0x1a2c8fa908>
```

We now examine the performances on new, unseen data, and store the prediction results on a pandas DataFrame. The results are quite good, as shown in the classification report: a precision of 80% is achieved as first attempt! This is remarkable, considering that we have no preprocessed the data as we did in all the methods seen in this book.

```
In [52]: y_pred = model.predict(X_test).astype(int)
         prediction_test = pd.DataFrame({
             "PassengerId": X_test["PassengerId"],
             "Survived": y_pred,
             "True": y_test.astype(int)
```

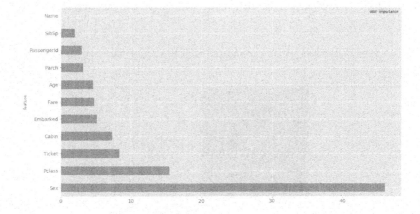

Figure 3.9: Global Feature Importance on the Training Titanic Dataset on fitting the catboost Classifier.

```
})

print(prediction_test.head())
```

```
     PassengerId  Survived  True
709          710         0     1
439          440         0     0
840          841         0     0
720          721         1     1
39            40         1     1
```

```
In [53]: print(classification_report(y_test, y_pred))
```

```
              precision    recall  f1-score   support

           0       0.81      0.88      0.84       105
           1       0.80      0.70      0.75        74

    accuracy                           0.80       179
   macro avg       0.80      0.79      0.79       179
weighted avg       0.80      0.80      0.80       179
```

The following snippet produce the confusion matrix on the test set, shown in Figure 3.10:

```
In [54]: classification_plots.confusion_matrix(y_test,y_pred)
```

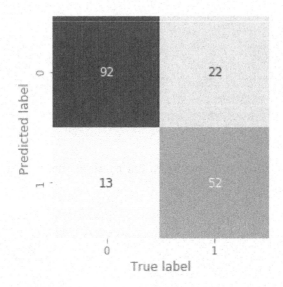

Figure 3.10: Confusion Matrix on the Titanic Test Set.

```
In [55]: preds_proba = model.predict_proba(X_test)
```

As a final remark, note that catboost works well in many situations, and therefore it is characterized by a variety of hyperparameters. In order to get the best performance from this algorithm, what is important is the choice of the parameters, and not necessarily their value via cross-validation. Among them, we mention the situations with:

1. Time-dependent features: if the value of one (or more) features changes drastically over time, it is advisable to set the hyperparameter has_time $=$ True;

2. Heterogeneity in the weight: there are real-life situations where recent data weight more than the older one. This is, for example, the case in pricing stock markets, or with longitudinal data, where the outcome strictly depends on the more recent set of features. With catboost, when you give more weightage to a particular example, this has a higher chance of getting selected in the random permutations. We could, for instance, assign a linear weightage all the datapoints by setting sample_weight $= [x \, for \, x$ in range(train.shape[0])]

3. Working with small datasets: when working with datasets with less than 50,000 examples, it is best practice to set the parametrer fold_len_multiplier as close as to 1 (must be >1) and approx_on_full_history =True . With these parameters, CatBoost calculates residuals for each data point using different model.

4. Working with large datasets: for large datasets, you can train CatBoost on GPUs by setting parameter task_type = GPU. It also supports multi-server distributed GPUs.

Chapter 4

An introduction to Modern Machine Learning Techniques

4.1 Introduction to Natural language Processing

In Natural Language Processing (NLP), we typically have to deal with text data, which notably comes from very heterogeneous resoures: for instance, it can be a document, where its content is grammatically correct and from which one might estract useful informations, such as topic extraction; it can also be a tweet, containing shorthands and hashtags, or a comment on youtube, from which we can perform sentiment analysis or text classification.

Such kind of data is obvioulsy unstructured, and therefore we need to perform very specific preprocessing to be able to fit a ML algorithm to a corpus of documents. For instance, it is important that we standardize these texts into a machine friendly format: we want our model to treat similar words semantically as the same. Consider the words *dog* and *dogs*: strictly speaking, they are different but they connotate the same thing. Moreover, the words *produce*, *produced* and *producing* should be standardized to the same root, regardless of their grammatical use and format.

The aim of this Section is to learn standard techniques that allow one to achieve this objective. Note that the text processing techniques one picks are strictly dependent on the application under investigation. The interest reader might refer to the well-written book by Bishop (2006) for further details, which is a nice and well-written reference for standard NLP techniques. In the last part of this section, we will focus on modern NLP approaches for similarity retrieval among a set of words and

115

documents, using Word2Vec and Doc2Vec, respectively.

```
In [1]: from egeaML import DataIngestion, nlp
        import csv
        import re
        import string
```

```
Using TensorFlow backend.
```

4.1.1   Preprocessing with Text Data

In general, when dealing with text data, we need to perform a rigorous text cleaning in order to extract useful information from the available raw, unstructured data: if we want to classify a document, we need to transform all the available data into numeric features, so that we could apply standard ML classifiers - otherwise the model is not able to ingest those data in that form. Here, we describe the standard preprocessing pipeline for text data, which consists of

1. **Tokenization**. Each row string - which might consists of a sentence or a whole document - is splitted into single, separated words, based on some user-defined rules, such as converting all words to lowercase, removing all stop and repeated words, as well as punctuactions.

2. **Lemmatization**. This process basically force a conjugate verb to be replaced by its simple form, e.g. *spoken* will be replaced by *speak*, as well as any transformation regarding third person.

3. **Stemmization**. Each single remaining word is reduced to its root form.

To do that, I will make use of the nltk library, proposed by Bird et al. (2009), which stands for natural language toolkit, though other libraries such as gensim can be used. Note that also the scikit-learn API can be exploited, with its CountVectorizer method, which is great especially if one aims to perform supervised learning based on extracted features with NLP techniques.

Tokenization is the process that turns a string or document into tokens, and this turns out to be the first step in preparing a text for NLP. Note that words such as *don't* will be splitted into two words after tokenization, that is *do* and *n't*, so we need to take care of contraction, punctualization and characters when doing this very important process.

There exists different theories and rules regarding tokenization, and you can create your own rules using regular expression: typically, we separate words by punctuation, or we just break out words or sentences. To perform tokenization, we use the nltk library, which stands for natural language toolkit.

Why bother with tokenization? Because it can helps us with some simple text processing tasks like mapping part of speech, matching common words, but it is also meant to clean the document by unwanted tokens, such as repeated words or punctuation. In particular, to perform tokenization, we use the simple_preprocess from gensim that performs the following operations:

1. it splits the sentence into single, lowercase tokens, and store them into a list;

2. it removes non-alphabethic characters, stopwords and even punctuations from that list;

Alternatively, the nltk library proposes different methods to perform tokenization, such as:

- the word_tokenize function returns a tokenized copy of the text under investigation ;

- the sent_tokenize tokenizes a document into sentences;

- the regexp_tokenize tokenizes a string or document based on a regular expression pattern.

The egeaML class nlp has a method called \textsf{simple_tokenization}, which performs similar steps as the one proposed above. As an example, let's consider the difference outputs of those different tokenization methods.

```
In [2]: mystr = "I haven't been to Rome (last year)-that's amazing!"
        tok_egeaML = nlp.simple_tokenization(mystr)
        tok_nltk = word_tokenize(mystr)
        tok_gensim = simple_preprocess(mystr)
        print('Original document: ', mystr)
        print('Tokenized list using the egeaML library: ', tok_egeaML)
        print('Tokenized list using the nltk library: ', tok_nltk)
        print('Tokenized list using the gensim library: ', tok_gensim)

Original document:  I haven't been to Rome (last year)-that's amazing!
```

```
Tokenized list using the egeaML library:  ['i', 'haven', 't', 'been',
'to', 'rome', 'last', 'year', 'that', 's', 'amazing']
```

```
Tokenized list using the nltk library:  ['I', 'have', "n't", 'been', 'to',
'Rome', '(', 'last', 'year', ')', '-', 'that', "'s", 'amazing', '!']
```

```
Tokenized list using the gensim library:  ['haven', 'been', 'to', 'rome',
'last', 'year', 'that', 'amazing']
```

We import a simple .txt document containing two small articles concerning a deep learning technique called Convolutional Neural Network.

```
In [3]: with open('article.txt') as f:
            reader = csv.reader(f)
            csv_rows = list(reader)
        text = ""
        for i in range(len(csv_rows[0])):
            text += csv_rows[0][i]
        text = text.split('\\n')
```

To show what sent_tokenization performs, we use the first article as an example:

```
In [4]: sentences = sent_tokenize(text[0])
        print(sentences)
```

```
['Convolutional neural networks are very general and very powerful.',
 'As an example consider Ilya Kostrikov and Tobias Weyand's ChronoNet a CNN that
  guesses the year in which a photo was taken.',
 'Since public sources can provide large numbers of digitally archived photos taken
  over the past century with known dates it's relatively straightforward to obtain
  labeled data (dated photos in this case) with which to train this network.']
```

Basically, it splits the article into paragraphs, where the full stop is the separator key between two sentences. On the contrary, word_tokenizer splits a document into single tokens, which definitely increases the granularity of the corpus.

```
In [5]: tokenized_sent = word_tokenize(sentences[2])
        print(tokenized_sent)
```

```
['Since', 'public', 'sources', 'can', 'provide', 'large', 'numbers', 'of',
 'digitally', 'archived', 'photos', 'taken', 'over', 'the', 'past', 'century', 'with',
```

```
'known', 'dates', 'it', ''', 's', 'relatively', 'straightforward', 'to', 'obtain',
'labeled', 'data', '(', 'dated', 'photos', 'in', 'this', 'case', ')', 'with',
'which', 'to', 'train', 'this', 'network', '.']
```

Note that we are still considering unwanted characters and words, such as the parentheses or the infinite marker "to" before a verb. However, removing stopwords and non-alphabetic characters is a very important preprocessing step. To do so, we might use book-specific class nlp, which has a method called parsing_text that basically removes the most common english stopwords, punctuactions and leading and trailing spaces.

```
In [6]: print(nlp.parsing_text(sentences[2]))
```

```
public sources provide large numbers digitally archived photos taken past century
known dates it's relatively straightforward obtain labeled data dated photos case
train network
```

Alternatively, one might define a a set of words that has to be removed before lemmization: this is typically made by all stopwords and punctuations.

```
In [7]: punct = set(string.punctuation)
        stop = set(stopwords.words('english'))
        stop.add('to')
```

To perform lemmatization and stemmization, we use the book-specific method clean_text from the egeaML library, which performs the following steps:

1. It firstly performs simple tokenization;

2. If the token is not a stopwords or its length is smaller than three, then we perform lemmatization and stemmization on that token;

3. else, it is removed.

Note that we use the Porter's algorithm (1980) named Snowball to perform stemmization, sicne it is the most popular one, and it has been shown to be empirically very effective (Manning et al. (2008)).

An example is made on the first document:

```
In [8]: doc_sample = text[0]
        print('Original document: \n')
```

```
        words = []
        for word in doc_sample.split(' '):
            words.append(word)
        print(words)
        print('\n Tokenized and lemmatized document: \n')
        print(nlp().clean_text(doc_sample))
```

Original document:

```
['Convolutional', 'neural', 'networks', 'are', 'very', 'general', 'and',
 'very', 'powerful.', 'As', 'an', 'example', 'consider', 'Ilya', 'Kostrikov',
 'and', 'Tobias', 'Weyand's', 'ChronoNet', 'a', 'CNN', 'that', 'guesses',
 'the', 'year', 'in', 'which', 'a', 'photo', 'was', 'taken.', 'Since',
 'public', 'sources', 'can', 'provide', 'large', 'numbers', 'of',
 'digitally', 'archived', 'photos', 'taken', 'over', 'the', 'past',
 'century', 'with', 'known', 'dates', 'it's', 'relatively', 'straightforward',
 'to', 'obtain', 'labeled', 'data', '(dated', 'photos', 'in', 'this', 'case)',
 'with', 'which', 'to', 'train', 'this', 'network.']
```

Tokenized and lemmatized document:

```
['convolut', 'neural', 'network', 'general', 'power', 'exampl', 'consid',
 'ilya', 'kostrikov', 'tobia', 'weyand', 'chrononet', 'cnn', 'guess',
 'year', 'photo', 'take', 'public', 'sourc', 'provid', 'larg', 'number',
 'digit', 'archiv', 'photo', 'take', 'past', 'centuri', 'know', 'date',
 'relat', 'straightforward', 'obtain', 'label', 'data', 'date', 'photo',
 'case', 'train', 'network']
```

The granularity of the document has been reduced by a large amount of charachters and stopwords, as desired. We now perform the same operation on the two articles:

In [9]: doc = [nlp().clean_text(x) for x in text]

Remark. *Twitter is a frequently used source for NLP tasks. We can extract useful information using regex, or the nltk class TweetTokenizer, which allows to parse easily tweets.*

To show how the TweetTokenizer works, let's take, for instance, a simple tweet:

```
In [10]: tweet = 'I used a kernelized SVM to classify text.
                  I love learning new #NLP techniques using #python!
                  @someone #NLP is real fun! :-) #ml #NLP #python'
```

```
In [11]: tweet
```

```
Out[11]: 'I used a kernelized SVM to classify text.
         I love learning new #NLP techniques using #python!
         @someone #NLP is real fun! :) #ml #NLP #python'
```

```
In [12]: tknzr = TweetTokenizer()
         tokens = tknzr.tokenize(tweet)
```

We can also tokenize the tweet by employing a regex that captures all the words that starts with a hashtag:

```
In [13]: regex = r"#\w+"
         list(set(regexp_tokenize(tweet, regex)))
```

```
Out[13]: ['#python', '#ml', '#NLP']
```

Notice that our pattern only matches words that start with a hashtag. Different regex can be used to crete different patterns, and I invite the interested reader to consult the following link for more details: https://docs.python.org/2/library/re.html.

4.1.2 Numerical Representation of Documents: the Bag-of-Words

Once we have reduced the original documents to a list of stems, it is possible to represent each single element as a unique integer: this can be easily done using the Dictionary object from gensim. In particular, the function doc2idx performs a ordered one-to-one mapping between words and integers. As an example, let's recall the first document we have processed before:

```
In [14]: print(doc[0])
```

```
['convolut', 'neural', 'network', 'general', 'power', 'exampl', 'consid',
 'ilya', 'kostrikov', 'tobia', 'weyand', 'chrononet', 'cnn', 'guess',
 'year', 'photo', 'take', 'public', 'sourc', 'provid', 'larg', 'number',
 'digit', 'archiv', 'photo', 'take', 'past', 'centuri', 'know', 'date',
 'relat', 'straightforward', 'obtain', 'label', 'data', 'date', 'photo',
 'case', 'train', 'network']
```

We would like to create a numerical representation of that list. This is easily implemented in gensim, as follows:

```
In [15]: dictionary = Dictionary(doc)
         print(dictionary.doc2idx(doc[0]))
```

```
[6, 19, 18, 11, 24, 10, 5, 13, 15, 31, 33, 3, 4, 12, 34, 23, 30, 26,
 28, 25, 17, 20, 9, 0, 23, 30, 22, 2, 14, 8, 27, 29, 21, 16, 7, 8, 23,
 1, 32, 18]
```

The interesting fact about the above representation is that it returns an ordered list of integers. But what does *ordered* mean in this context? For instance, the word *network* appears now as the integer 18, and it occurrs twice. This representation therefore is just a mapping, in the sense it preserves the order in which each word appears in the list, but it does not perform any aggregation of the numerical elements inside the list of tokens. If one is interested in this task, then he has to focus on its corresponding bag-of-words representation.

The bag-of-words representation for texts was proposed by Harris (1954) as a feature to represent texts as a fixed-length feature vector. The bag-of-words representation (BoW, shortly) simply counts the absolute frequency of each word within a document. This representaton is extremely useful, since many ML algorithm requires the input to be represented as a fixed-length vector. Computing the BoW representation for a corpus of documents consists of the following three steps:

1. **Tokenization**. Split each document into tokens by splitting them on whitespace and punctuation.

2. **Vocabulary building**. Build a vocabulary of all words that appear in the corpus of documents, and order them in alphabetical order.

3. **Encoding**. For each document, compute the words absolute frequency.

These steps are performed by the doc2bow function, as shown in the next snippet:

```
In [16]: corpus = [dictionary.doc2bow(x) for x in doc]
```

```
In [17]: print(corpus[0])
```

```
[(0, 1), (1, 1), (2, 1), (3, 1), (4, 1), (5, 1), (6, 1), (7, 1),
 (8, 2), (9, 1), (10, 1), (11, 1), (12, 1), (13, 1), (14, 1),
 (15, 1), (16, 1), (17, 1), (18, 2), (19, 1), (20, 1), (21, 1),
 (22, 1), (23, 3), (24, 1), (25, 1), (26, 1), (27, 1), (28, 1),
 (29, 1), (30, 2), (31, 1), (32, 1), (33, 1), (34, 1)]
```

We can generate a frequency matrix containing the number of times a word appeared in each of the stemmed documents. Basically, each row represents a document, and columns are the words contained in the corpus. In gensim, this is generated using the method corpus2dense.

```
In [18]: mylist = list()
            for k,v in dictionary.token2id.items():
                mylist.append(k)


            doc2freq = pd.DataFrame(matutils.corpus2dense(corpus,
                    num_terms=len(dictionary.token2id)),
                    index = mylist,
                    columns=['Doc1', 'Doc2'])


            doc2freq.T.iloc[:,10:20]
```

```
Out[18]:      exampl general guess ilya know kostrikov label larg network \
         Doc1    1.0     1.0    1.0  1.0  1.0       1.0   1.0  1.0     2.0
         Doc2    0.0     0.0    0.0  0.0  0.0       0.0   0.0  0.0     1.0


              neural
         Doc1    1.0
         Doc2    1.0
```

Remark. *If interested in getting a dense BoW representation of the corpus, gensim allows you to get it easily, as follows.*

```
In [19]: tf_sparse_array = matutils.corpus2csc(corpus)
            tf_sparse_array
```

```
Out[19]: <63x2 sparse matrix of type '<class 'numpy.float64'>'
            with 69 stored elements in Compressed Sparse Column format>
```

Note that the scikit-learn function CountVectorizer allows to produce a BoW representation of the given corpus. This function is a transformer, and it will take a series of arguments; we just used some of them, which are described here:

- min_df: minimum required number of occurences of a word;
- stop_words: removes the unwanted words;
- lowercase: converts all words to lowercase;

- token_pattern: selects only words with a minimum number of characters of two.

```
In [20]: vectorizer = CountVectorizer(analyzer='word',
                                       min_df=2,
                                       stop_words='english',
                                       lowercase=True,
                                       token_pattern='[a-zA-Z0-9]{2,}',
                                       )

         data_vectorized = vectorizer.fit_transform(text)
         data_dense = data_vectorized.todense()
```

Note that despite its popularity, the BoW has many disadvantages. On the one hand, the ordering of tokens is completely lost, which implies that differnt sentences might have the same numerical representation. on the other hand, BoW tend to ignore semantics of the words, that is the distance between two (or more) words. We will discuss alternative representations in Section 4.1.6.

4.1.3 Practical Example: Sentiment Analysis with IMDb Reviews Dataset

Let us try to perform a simple binary text classification on the avialble dataset IMDb Reviews on movie review (which is available at: http://ai.stanford.edu/ amaas/data/sentiment/).

the IMDb dataset was firstly proposed by Maas et al. (2011) as a benchmark for sentiment analysis, and it consists of 100,000 movie reviews taken from the website IMDB. The task is as follows: given a review, we want to classify the movie as *good* or *negative* based on the review content. To do so, we need to convert the data, that is we need to convert the string representation of the text into a numeric representation that we can apply our standard machine learning pipeline to classify movies.

To download the dataset, we can use the utility functionality provided in the egeaML library, which allows to download easily the .tar file containing the IMDB movie reviews. In case the data have already been downloaded, the report will inform the user about that (as shown below).

```
In [21]: url = 'http://ai.stanford.edu/~amaas/data/sentiment/aclImdb_v1.tar.gz'
         foldername = 'aclImdb'
```

```
In [22]: utils = utils()
         utils.download_data(foldername, urls=[url])


Downloading data...
aclImdb_v1.tar.gz already downloaded


Download Finished


In [23]: from sklearn.datasets import load_files
         reviews_train = load_files("aclImdb/train/")
         text_train, y_train = reviews_train.data, reviews_train.target
         reviews_test = load_files("aclImdb/test/")
         text_test, y_test = reviews_test.data, reviews_test.target

In [24]: vect = CountVectorizer(min_df=5,
                      stop_words='english').fit(text_train)
         X_train = vect.transform(text_train)
```

With the CountVectorizer we have created a (sparse) matrix, which is a numerical representation of the text data we have. From this, we can now apply any ML model we wish.

```
In [25]: feature_names = vect.get_feature_names()

In [26]: scores = cross_val_score(LogisticRegression(),
                          X_train, y_train, cv=5)
         print("Mean cross-validation accuracy: {:.2f}".format(
                          np.mean(scores)))

Mean cross-validation accuracy: 0.88

In [27]:param_grid = {'C': [0.001, 0.01, 0.1, 1, 10]}
         grid = GridSearchCV(LogisticRegression(), param_grid, cv=5)
         grid.fit(X_train, y_train)
         print("Best cross-validation score: {:.2f}".format(
                          grid.best_score_))
         print("Best parameters: ", grid.best_params_)

Best cross-validation score: 0.88
Best parameters:  {'C': 0.1}
```

A simple Logistic Regression has an accuracy of 88% with this set of data: amazing! Interestingly, we have very good performances also on the test set.

```
In [28]: X_test = vect.transform(text_test)
         print("{:.2f}".format(grid.score(X_test, y_test)))
```

0.87

4.1.4   Term Frequency-Inverse Document Frequency

BoW can be a great way to determine the significant words in a text, based on the number of times they are used. However, the above frequency matrix does not take into account the importance of each single word within a document. In other words, it tends to give more importance to popular words, and less to contextual words. Instead, the term frequency-inverse document frequency matrix (tf-idf, shortly) allows to weight each word based on its frequency in the document. But how does it work? Basically, the weight of a term that occurs in a document is simply proportional to the term frequency. More formally, for a term i in document j, we compute its weight as follows:

$$ w_{ij} = \text{tf}_{ij} \cdot \log \left(\frac{N}{\text{df}_i} \right) $$

where

- tf_{ij} describes the number of occurrences of word i in document j;

- df_i describes the number of documents containing i;

- N denotes the number of documents.

Practically, higher scores are associated with words that are specific to a particular document, and that are mostly used there. Instead, lower scores will be assigned to words that frequently appear in different documents. Hence, higher scores are associated to words that are particularly relevant for that particular document.

Note that differently from BoW, where we have d-dimensional vectors of discrete counts, the tf-idf matrix will instead contains continuous values. Let's see how to produce a tf-idf matrix in gensim, using the function TfidfModel from the models class.

```
In [29]: tfidf = models.TfidfModel(corpus)
```

To show the most important words for a particular document, we use the book-specific function top_words:

```
In [30]: nlp.top_words(corpus=corpus, dictionary=dictionary,
                       doc=corpus[0], n_words=10)
```

```
Out[30]: ['photo (0.474)',
          'date (0.316)',
          'archiv (0.158)',
          'case (0.158)',
          'centuri (0.158)',
          'chrononet (0.158)',
          'consid (0.158)',
          'digit (0.158)',
          'exampl (0.158)',
          'general (0.158)']
```

We can store the results in a dataframe, as we have done for the BoW representation.

```
In [31]: tfidf_mat = pd.DataFrame(matutils.corpus2dense(
                     [tfidf[x] for x in corpus],
                     num_terms=len(dictionary.token2id)),
                     index = mylist,
                     columns=['Doc1', 'Doc2'])

         tfidf_mat.iloc[30:40, :].T
```

```
Out[31]:      take      tobia     train    weyand        year  breakthrough      build  \
        Doc1   0.0  0.158114  0.158114  0.158114  0.158114      0.000000   0.000000
        Doc2   0.0  0.000000  0.000000  0.000000  0.000000      0.149071   0.149071


               classif      come  constitut
        Doc1  0.000000  0.000000   0.000000
        Doc2  0.149071  0.149071   0.149071
```

4.1.5 Bag-of-Words with More Than One Word (n-Grams)

Let's consider the follwing two strings:

- it's boring, not fun at all

- it's fun, not boring at all

For a human being, those two strings are obviously different, but for a machine they share the same structure! This translates into the fact that a machine is not able to distinguish their meaning, and therefore one of them would be missclassified. What we want to stress is that the two BoW representations are exactly the same, but the original texts have a different meaning. Hence, BoW representation has a drawback: it looses completely the order in which the words are given in the sentence. Luckily, we can capture the impact of a word's neighborhood by taking into account not just single tokens but also the counts of pairs (bigrams) or triplets (trigrams) of words that appear next to each other. More generally, sequences of n tokens are known as *n-grams*.

With the scikit-learn CountVectorizer we can change the range of tokens that are considered as features by changing the ngram_range parameter, which is a tuple consisting of the minimum and the maximum length of the sequences of tokens that we wish to consider. We fit a Logistic Regression model on the IMDb dataset, taking into acount different n_gram range, as follows:

```
In [32]: pipe = make_pipeline(CountVectorizer(min_df=5),
                              LogisticRegression())
         param_grid = {
         "logisticregression__C": [0.001, 0.01, 0.1, 1, 10, 100],
         "countvectorizer__ngram_range": [(1, 1), (1, 2), (1, 3)]}
         grid = GridSearchCV(pipe, param_grid, cv=5)
         grid.fit(text_train, y_train)
         print("Best cross-validation score: {:.2f}".format(
                              grid.best_score_))
         print("Best parameters:\n{}".format(grid.best_params_))

Best cross-validation score: 0.91
Best parameters:
{'logisticregression__C': 100, 'countvectorizer__ngram_range': (1, 3)}
```

We have slightly imporoved the model, compared to a simple BoW model. To better understand the motivation of using n-grams, let's try to play a little bit with the following set of sentences:

```
In [33]: documents = [
                "Apple stock has recently hit new all-time highs.",
                "A recent research has shown that an apple a day is a good ally
                to prevent cancer formation.",
                "Apple has recently launched a new iphone",
                "I prefer eating oranges instead of apples in the winter.",
```

```
                    "scikit-learn logo is orange and blue.",
                    "scikit-learn pipeline object is fantastic"]

In [34]:vect = CountVectorizer(stop_words='english')
        vect.fit(documents)

Out[34]: CountVectorizer(analyzer='word', binary=False, decode_error='strict',
                    dtype=<class 'numpy.int64'>, encoding='utf-8',
                    input='content', lowercase=True, max_df=1.0,
                    max_features=None, min_df=1, ngram_range=(1, 1),
                    preprocessor=None, stop_words='english',
                    strip_accents=None,
                    token_pattern='(?u)\\b\\w\\w+\\b',
                    tokenizer=None, vocabulary=None)
```

Fitting the CountVectorizer consists of the tokenization of the training data and building of the vocabulary, which we can access as the vocabulary_ attribute:

```
In [35]: print("Vocabulary size: {}".format(len(vect.vocabulary_)))
        print("Vocabulary content:\n {}".format(vect.vocabulary_))

Vocabulary size: 30
Vocabulary content:
 {'apple': 1, 'stock': 27, 'recently': 23, 'hit': 10, 'new': 16, 'time': 28,
  'highs': 9, 'recent': 22, 'research': 24, 'shown': 26, 'day': 4, 'good': 8,
  'ally': 0, 'prevent': 21, 'cancer': 3, 'formation': 7, 'launched': 13,
  'iphone': 12, 'prefer': 20, 'eating': 5, 'orange': 18, 'instead': 11,
  'winter': 29, 'scikit': 25, 'learn': 14, 'logo': 15, 'blue': 2,
  'pipeline': 19, 'object': 17, 'fantastic': 6}
```

To create the Bag-of-Words representation for the training data, we call the transform method:

```
In [36]: bag_of_words = vect.transform(documents)
        print("bag_of_words: {}".format(repr(bag_of_words)))
        print("Dense representation of bag_of_words:\n{}".format(
                        bag_of_words.toarray()))

bag_of_words: <6x30 sparse matrix of type '<class 'numpy.int64'>'
        with 38 stored elements in Compressed Sparse Row format>
Dense representation of bag_of_words:
```

```
[[0 1 0 0 0 0 0 0 1 1 0 0 0 0 0 1 0 0 0 0 0 0 1 0 0 0 1 1 0]
 [1 1 0 1 1 0 0 1 1 0 0 0 0 0 0 0 0 0 0 0 1 1 0 1 0 1 0 0 0]
 [0 1 0 0 0 0 0 0 0 0 0 0 1 1 0 0 1 0 0 0 0 0 1 0 0 0 0 0 0]
 [0 1 0 0 0 1 0 0 0 0 0 1 0 0 0 0 0 0 1 0 1 0 0 0 0 0 0 0 1]
 [0 0 1 0 0 0 0 0 0 0 0 0 0 0 1 1 0 0 1 0 0 0 0 0 1 0 0 0 0]
 [0 0 0 0 0 0 1 0 0 0 0 0 0 0 1 0 0 1 0 1 0 1 0 0 0 0 1 0 0 0 0]]
```

Note that the columns of the above co-occurrence matrix are orthogonal, but we can still compute the similarity of two sentences using the tfidf matrix. Hence, we compute it using the TfidfVectorizer method, as follows:

```
In [37]: from sklearn.feature_extraction.text import TfidfVectorizer
         tf = TfidfVectorizer(stop_words='english')
```

To compute the similarity between sentences, we perform tfidf matrix multiplication, as follows:

```
In [38]: tfidf = tf.fit_transform(documents)
         pairwise_similarity = tfidf * tfidf.T
         pairwise_similarity.toarray()
```

```
Out[38]: array([[1.         , 0.04821943, 0.36974535, 0.06578578, 0.         ,
                 0.         ],
                [0.04821943, 1.         , 0.05985831, 0.05134479, 0.         ,
                 0.         ],
                [0.36974535, 0.05985831, 1.         , 0.08166472, 0.         ,
                 0.         ],
                [0.06578578, 0.05134479, 0.08166472, 1.         , 0.14967046,
                 0.         ],
                [0.         , 0.         , 0.         , 0.14967046, 1.         ,
                 0.32189934],
                [0.         , 0.         , 0.         , 0.         , 0.32189934,
                 1.         ]])
```

What we see is that there is an interesting similarity between the first and third sentence (that is the ones which speak about the Apple company), as well as between the last two sentences (which speak about the scikit-learn project). To look only at bigrams—that is, only at sequences of two tokens following each other—we can set ngram_range to (2, 2):

```
In [39]: cv = CountVectorizer(ngram_range=(1, 3)).fit(documents)
         print("Vocabulary size: {}".format(len(cv.vocabulary_)))
         print("Vocabulary:\n{}".format(cv.get_feature_names()))
```

Vocabulary size: 127
Vocabulary:
['all', 'all time', 'all time highs', 'ally', 'ally to', 'ally to prevent',
 'an', 'an apple', 'an apple day', 'an apple in', 'an orange',
 'an orange instead', 'and', 'and blue', 'apple', 'apple day',
 'apple day is', 'apple has', 'apple has recently', 'apple in',
 'apple in the', 'apple stock', 'apple stock has', 'blue', 'cancer',
 'cancer formation', 'day', 'day is', 'day is good', 'eating',
 'eating an', 'eating an orange', 'fantastic', 'formation', 'good',
 'good ally', 'good ally to', 'has', 'has recently', 'has recently hit',
 'has recently launched', 'has shown', 'has shown that', 'highs', 'hit',
 'hit new', 'hit new all', 'in', 'in the', 'in the winter', 'instead',
 'instead of', 'instead of an', 'iphone', 'is', 'is fantastic', 'is good',
 'is good ally', 'is orange', 'is orange and', 'launched', 'launched new',
 'launched new iphone', 'learn', 'learn logo', 'learn logo is',
 'learn pipeline', 'learn pipeline object', 'logo', 'logo is',
 'logo is orange', 'new', 'new all', 'new all time', 'new iphone',
 'object', 'object is', 'object is fantastic', 'of', 'of an', 'of an apple',
 'orange', 'orange and', 'orange and blue', 'orange instead',
 'orange instead of', 'pipeline', 'pipeline object', 'pipeline object is',
 'prefer', 'prefer eating', 'prefer eating an', 'prevent',
 'prevent cancer', 'prevent cancer formation', 'recent',
 'recent research', 'recent research has', 'recently', 'recently hit',
 'recently hit new', 'recently launched', 'recently launched new',
 'research', 'research has', 'research has shown', 'scikit',
 'scikit learn', 'scikit learn logo', 'scikit learn pipeline', 'shown',
 'shown that', 'shown that an', 'stock', 'stock has',
 'stock has recently', 'that', 'that an', 'that an apple', 'the',
 'the winter', 'time', 'time highs', 'to', 'to prevent',
 'to prevent cancer', 'winter']
```

Using longer sequences of tokens usually results in many more features, and in more specific features. Let's see how the similarity matrix has changed after having choosen to use also biagrams:

```
In [40]: tf_bg = TfidfVectorizer(stop_words='english',ngram_range=(1, 2))
         tf_bg.fit(documents)
```
```

Interestingly, considering bigrams does not lead to an improvement in the information retriveal in this set of docuemnts.

```
In [41]: tfidf_bg = tf_bg.fit_transform(documents)
         pairwise_similarity = tfidf_bg * tfidf_bg.T
         pairwise_similarity.toarray()

Out[41]: array([[1.         , 0.02402227, 0.17883097, 0.03250323, 0.         ,
                0.         ],
               [0.02402227, 1.         , 0.02961369, 0.0259489 , 0.         ,
                0.         ],
               [0.17883097, 0.02961369, 1.         , 0.04006867, 0.         ,
                0.         ],
               [0.03250323, 0.0259489 , 0.04006867, 1.         , 0.0765878 ,
                0.         ],
               [0.         , 0.         , 0.         , 0.0765878 , 1.         ,
                0.25691906],
               [0.         , 0.         , 0.         , 0.         , 0.25691906,
                1.         ]])
```

For most applications, the minimum number of tokens should be one, as single
words often capture a lot of meaning. Adding bigrams helps in most cases, but
longer sequences might lead to overfitting. As a thumb rule, the number of bigrams
could be the number of unigrams squared and the number of trigrams could be the
number of unigrams to the power of three, leading to very large feature spaces.

4.1.6   Beyond Bag-of-words: Word Embeddings

The methods we have investigated so far typically use a local representation of the
word, meaning that each sentence is encoded into a discrete vector of occurrences
(typically 1 if the word was observed in that document, 0 otherwise), which gives
to us a very sparse vector with dimension corresponding to the words in the corpus
of documents. Based on that representation, we have discussed the tf-idf representation, which basically is a continuous representation of the discrete counts, taking
into account the corresponding weight in the document.

This was the standard approach to represent documents in terms of fixed-length
vector representation. But, as we have already seen in previous sections, the BoW
approach suffers from (at least) two problems: on the one hand, we hand up with
extremely long, sparse vectors, which might be a problem for the RAM as the size
of the corpus gets biggere and bigger. On the other hand, the column vector of the

co-occurrence matrix are completely orthogonal, and therefore we might not be able to retrieve similarity relationship between them.

A possible solution is to represent each single word as a dense vector of d-dimensions, which is also referred as distributed representation (or simply embeddings): the idea is that each word is going to be represented by a dense fixed-length vector that contains the essence of that word, chosen so that it is similar to vectors of words that appear in similar contexts. Since the seminal work by Hinton et al. (1986), many interesting works have been produced based on that idea. Among many, it is worth to cite the paper by Socher et al. (2011) and Glorot et al. (2011). One of the most interesting works produced in the last decade is the paper by Mikolov et al. (2013), who introduced the Skip-gram model, which is an efficient model that allows to learn the word vectors based on their contextual words. This paper basically extends the idea by Bengio et al. (2006), who actually used the concatenation of several word vectors as the input of a neural network, and tried to predict the next word based on that augmented vector. However, differently from their structure, the training of the Skip-gram model is somehow lighter, since we end up with a binary classification task, and it does not involve dense matrix multiplications.

The skip-gram algorithm is one of two algorithms proposed by Mikolov et al. (2013a and 2013b), and we typically refer to this class of algorithms as Word2Vec. The intuition of Word2Vec is that instead of counting how often each word w occurs near another one (in the corpus), we train a supervised model which target is the one-hot representation of the word w.

The algorithm basically works as follows: each word in the dictionary is represented by a vector, which is randomly initialized. Then, for each word w in the given text, we are going to compute the similarity between its word vector and the context words vectors; based on that similarity, we then calculate the probability that the context word is going to be associated with the word w, and we iteratively adjust the initial vector using gradient descent, that is we adjust the word vectors to maximize the following probability:

$$\mathbb{P}\left(c|w,\theta\right) = \frac{e^{u_c^T \cdot v_w}}{\sum_{v \in V} e^{u_v^T \cdot v_w}}$$

where v_w denotes the word vector when w is the center word we start with, and u_w is instead the word vector when w is a context word, and the set V denotes the entire set of tokens in the corpus. Note that θ denotes a vector of parameters (in our case word vectors) that we wish to optimize, which dimension is going to be

$2dV$, where d is the dimension of the embedding, V the dimension of the tokenized corpus, and since we are considering, for each word, its vector when it is a center or context word, we multiply by two. Under the assumption that all context words are independent, and taking into account multiple context words in the window of size m, we therefore maximize the following loglikelihood function:

$$\frac{1}{T} \sum_{t=1}^{T} \sum_{-m \leq j \leq j} \log \mathbb{P}\left(w_{t+j} | w_t, \theta\right) \tag{4.1}$$

where T denotes the length of the corpus. The goal is to minimize the above cost function, which translates as the model is going to predict, given some context, the word that semantically is more appropriate. How do we compute those probabilities? During the training phase, the skip-gram tries to adjust the parameters to minimize the cost function. Typically, this is done by computing all vector gradients for the vector parameter θ, which basically contains the word vector representation. The calculations are shown in Appendix B to avoid mathematics during the exposition.

Let us see in practice why Word2Vec embeddings have gained such a remarkable popularity.

```
In [42]: from egeaML import *
         import gensim.downloader as api
```

Using TensorFlow backend.

The following application has been inspired by the following gensim stable documentation at https://radimrehurek.com/gensim/models/keyedvectors.html. In particular, we will make use of the pre-trained GloVe Wikipedia word vectors (see Pennington et al. (2014) for furher details, and also refer to the stable GloVe website: https://nlp.stanford.edu/projects/glove/). Note that gensim easily allow to load the Glove dataset into Word2Vec format using its downloader object, as shown here. Otherwise, the reader can download the data from the aforementioned website, and convert the file into the Word2Vec format using the method glove2word2vec from the scripts class.

```
In [43]: model = api.load('glove-wiki-gigaword-100')
```

Let us try to see to which terms *Italy* is related:

```
In [44]: model.most_similar('italy')

Out[44]: [('spain', 0.7746186852455139),
          ('italian', 0.7569283246994019),
          ('portugal', 0.7421526312828064),
          ('germany', 0.740085244178772),
          ('greece', 0.7235244512557983),
          ('netherlands', 0.7212409973144531),
          ('france', 0.7163637280464172),
          ('austria', 0.7158598899841309),
          ('switzerland', 0.6981543302536011),
          ('brazil', 0.6805199384689331)]
```

That makes sense: the country *Italy* is mostly related to European countries, as well as to the word that identifies its citizens. That was easy: let us try with another one.

```
In [45]: model.most_similar('schumacher')

Out[45]: [('barrichello', 0.8159974813461304),
          ('ralf', 0.8043726682662964),
          ('ferrari', 0.8011481761932373),
          ('coulthard', 0.8001769781112671),
          ('massa', 0.7799736261367798),
          ('raikkonen', 0.7790895700454712),
          ('alonso', 0.7785213589668274),
          ('montoya', 0.7640366554260254),
          ('villeneuve', 0.7573407888412476),
          ('mclaren', 0.7414728403091431)]
```

Not surprisingly, the word *Schumacher* is related to many other famous F1 drivers. For those who are not keen on F1, those famous names of the first decade of the current century. Let us try a last one:

```
In [46]: model.most_similar('apple')

Out[46]: [('microsoft', 0.7449405789375305),
          ('ibm', 0.6821643710136414),
          ('intel', 0.6778088212013245),
```

```
('software', 0.6775422096252441),
('dell', 0.6741442680358887),
('pc', 0.6678153276443481),
('macintosh', 0.66175377368927),
('iphone', 0.6595611572265625),
('ipod', 0.6534676551818848),
('hewlett', 0.6516579985618591)]
```

That one is tricky, since it might be referred to Apple company, but also to the forbidden fruit. Another interesting application is based on the concept of vectors' analogy, proposed by Levy and Goldberg (2014), who actually show that the difference between vectors can capture some analogies between words. For instance, they show that if we consider the difference in (capital,country) vectors of a specific country, say (Rome, Italy), and we take the vector of France, then

$$v(\text{Rome}) - v(\text{Italy}) + v(\text{France})$$

results in the vector of Paris. That is amazing, isn't it? To convince the reader about this amazing relationship, consider the following examples:

```
In [47]: nlp = nlp()
         nlp.analogy(model,'italy','denmark','rome')
```

```
Out[47]: 'copenhagen'
```

```
In [48]: nlp.analogy(model,'spain','netherlands','madrid')
```

```
Out[48]: 'amsterdam'
```

Note that the embedding has associated to the Netherlands the city Amsterdam: in principle, that is correct, but that would be wrong if we were to consider capitals. Another example is the following one, which perfectly shows a good match between animals and food:

```
In [10]: nlp.analogy(model,'banana', 'cheese', 'monkey')
```

```
Out[10]: 'goat'
```

As a final exercise, let us try to plot a list of words based on their similarity values obtained from the embeddings. This can be easily done using the egeaML object display_similarity, which performs PCA for dimensionality reduction, and takes two

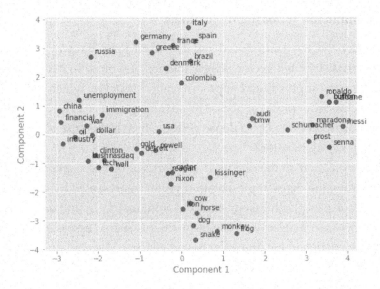

Figure 4.1: Clusters of selected words, based on their similarity retrived by the Word2Vec model.

arguments: the model and the list of words we are interested in. Results are shown in Figure 4.1. We clearly see there is a cluster made by all countries, and closer countries seem to be geographically related as well. Another interesting cluster is the one on the left, which can be identified as the one related to political and economical events. On the right, instead, we clearly identify famous sportsmen. A little remark on the words *usa* and *china*: they are not fully clustered as country, since they seem to be strictly related to the cluster we defined as related to political and economical events. This makes sense, since those two countries are the two biggest economy in the world.

```
In [5]: mywordlist = ['powell', 'russia', 'colombia', 'audi', 'bmw',
                      'ronaldo', 'nasdaq', 'clinton', 'nixon', 'reagan',
                      'bush', 'kissinger', 'carter', 'messi', 'maradona',
                      'immigration', 'greece', 'buffon', 'schumacher',
                      'italy', 'france', 'usa', 'germany', 'china', 'prost',
                      'senna', 'buffon', 'war', 'zidane', 'dollar',
                      'gold','oil', 'unemployment', 'brazil', 'snake','wall',
                      'tech', 'financial', 'industry', 'detroit','horse',
                      'lion', 'monkey', 'frog', 'dog', 'cow',
                      'spain', 'denmark']

        nlp.display_similarity(model, mywordlist)
```

Paragraph Continuous Vector Representations

In this subsection, we have introduced and discussed a popular way to learn continuos fixed-length distributed vector representations of words. In 2014, Mikolov and Le proposed a more sophisticated approach, called *Doc2Vec*, which allows to learn distributed vectors from pieces of texts. The advantage of using Doc2Vec is that each document is now represented by a dense vector, which is then use to predict words, or to perform text classification.

The idea is very similar to the one used in *Word2Vec* but here, every paragraph is mapped into a unique dense representation vector, represented by a concatenation between a unique paragraph token, extracted from matrix D, and word vectors extracted from the word matrix W. While the former is shared across all words generated from the same document, the latter is shared across documents.

We will not go into the details of this interesting model, so please refer to the aforementioned paper for further details. In the following, we will briefly discuss this methodology based on a toy example.

```
In [6]: import csv
        import random
        from gensim.models.doc2vec import Doc2Vec, TaggedDocument
        from egeaML import nlp
```

Using TensorFlow backend.

We read some data, created *ad hoc* for this illustration. You find it on the data folder in the book-specific GitHub repository, under the name doc2vecdocs.txt. We read the file, and create a list of paragraphs from it.

```
In [7]: with open('doc2vec_docs.txt') as f:
            reader = csv.reader(f, delimiter='.')
            csv_rows = list(reader)
        docs = [item for sublist in csv_rows for item in sublist]
```

For each paragraph document, we perform the usual cleaning before feeding it into the model. Note that Doc2Vec requires each document to be represented as a concatenation between its corresponding words vectors and its paragraph token, so we create a list of tagged documents, using the egeaML method tagging_doc2vec, which returns a list of tagged words, one for each document.

```
In [8]: doc = [nlp().clean_text(x) for x in docs]
        tagged = nlp().tagging_doc2vec(doc)
```

We now fit the Doc2Vec model, using the function Doc2Vec from gensim. Here the parameter vector_size stands for the the length of the feature vector representation, window describes the maximum distance between the current and predicted word within a paragraph, min_count ignores all words with total frequency lower than the provided number, and epochs describes the number of iterations over the corpus of documents.

```
In [9]:  model = Doc2Vec(vector_size=100, window=10, min_count=2,
                                         workers=-1, epochs=10)
         model.build_vocab(tagged)
         model.train(tagged, total_examples=model.corpus_count,
                            epochs=model.epochs)
```

As a use-case, we perform similarity retrieval between documents, based on the distributed representations of the training documents. Note that one might take unseen data, and try to retrieve the same similarity on it. This means that the inferred vector is going to be the new document in the required format (i.e. splitted list of preprocessed words).

```
In [10]:  id = random.randint(0, len(tagged)-1)
          inferred_vector = model.infer_vector(tagged[id].words)
          similarities = model.docvecs.most_similar([inferred_vector],
                               topn=len(model.docvecs))
```

```
In [11]: print(' Most Similar Documents with Document %s which text is:\n %s\n' % (id,
                                docs[id]))
            for label, index in [('TOP SIMILAR', 0),
                                 ('SECOND MOST SIMILAR', 1),
                                 ('THIRD MOST SIMILAR', 2),]:
               print('%s %s:\n «%s»\n' % (label, similarities[index],
                             ''.join(docs[similarities[index][0]])))

Most Similar Documents with Document 118 which text is:
The more data that is fed into it - whether images of terrorist insignia or
harmful keywords - the more the machine learning technology learns and improves


TOP SIMILAR (27, 0.22756348550319672):
« Typically, the generative network learns to map from a latent space to a data
distribution of interest, while the discriminative network distinguishes candidates
produced by the generator from the true data distribution»


SECOND MOST SIMILAR (75, 0.2103119045495987):
« Deep learning based on superficial features is decidedly not a tool
that should be deployed to ''accelerate'' criminal justice;
```

```
attempts to do so, like Faception's, will instead perpetuate injustice»
```

```
THIRD MOST SIMILAR (119, 0.1768016815185547):
 « Without enough training data, the system does not know what to look for»
```

Interestingly, the model has learnt that we are speaking about a topic related to machine learning, more specifically to image recognition, and therefore he has returned the similarity with a document that speaks about GANs (top similar), a document that speaks about criminality and Faception, which is a facial personality analytics technology company (second similar), and finally to a generic paragraph related to machine learning model's training.

4.2   Introduction to Deep Learning

In the last ten years, deep learning has become somehow a buzzword in the machine learning community, sometimes extremely abused, but generally most of the practitioners do not even know what this term means! Notably, they tend to wrongly separate the two fields, although we should highlight that they are strongly related to each other. Generally speaking, with the term deep learning we indeed refer to a branch of machine learning that typically deals with artificial neural networks, such as the one represented in Figure 4.2.

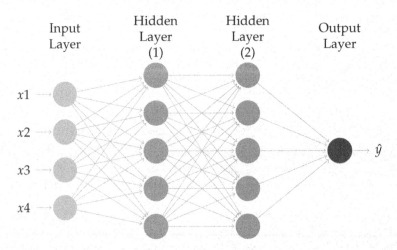

Figure 4.2: Representation of a Neural Network Architecture with two hidden layers.

More specifically, a deep learning mode is a machine learning algorithm that takes in, as input, a features vector **X** used to predict the dependent variable y. Hence, it is a supervised learning model but works differently from the models we have seen so far. Their structure is made of three main components, which are referred as

- the input layer, which takes in a numerical representation of the data;

- the hidden layer, where computations take place, and which plays the role of black-box inside the model, and

- the output layers, which outputs the predictions of the model.

We will not deep into the structure of artificial neural networks here: the interested reader might refer to the book of Courville et al. (2017) or the one by Chollet (2017) to deep the theory and structure behind this family of algorithm.

The aim of this Section is to introduce the reader to a simple application of deep learning using the Keras API, firstly proposed by Chollet et al. (2015) and nowadays available with the stable release 2.2.4. Keras is a high-level neural networks API, capable of running on top of Tensorflow, Theano, or CNTK. It is one of the most user-friendly API for deep learning, and it can also be run on both CPU and GPU. Please refer to the available documentation to properly install it using pip or conda: https://keras.io.

```
In [1]: import pandas as pd
        import numpy as np
        import seaborn as sns
        import matplotlib.pyplot as plt
        from egeaML import neural_network
        from sklearn.metrics import classification_report
        from sklearn.datasets import make_classification, make_circles
```

Using TensorFlow backend.

```
In [2]: #keras modules
        from keras.models import Sequential
        from keras.layers import Dense,Dropout, BatchNormalization, Activation
        from keras.optimizers import Adam
        from keras.callbacks import EarlyStopping
        from keras.utils.np_utils import to_categorical
```

Let us begin with a very simple example: a dataset linearly separable in two classes. This is a very simple binry classification task, and we would like to solve it using the deep learning architecture.

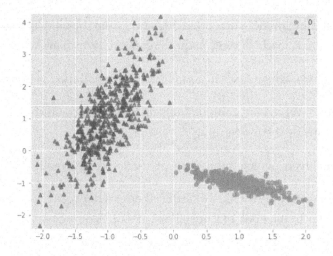

Figure 4.3: A linear separable dataset for Classification.

```
In [3]: X, y = make_classification(n_samples=1000, n_features=2,
                                    n_redundant=0, n_informative=2,
                                    random_state=7,
                                    n_clusters_per_class=1)
        neural_network.plot_data(X,y)
```

The easiest way of creating a model in Keras is by using the sequential API, which allows you to stack one layer on top of the other. Since our toy example shows a clear linear decision boundary between the two classes, let us try to fit a simple Logistic Regression model: in this case, we will have the input nodes directly connected to output node, without any hidden layers. Once the class Sequential is initialized, we start adding layer using the Dense function in Keras, which constructs a fully connected neural network layer. The function arguments are defined as follows:

- units: it represents the dimensionality of the output space;

- input_shape: it is the starting tensor ingested into the first hidden layer. This must have the same shape as your training data, that is two.

Note that only the first layer in Keras models need to specify the input dimensions. The subsequent layers do not need to specify this argument because Keras can infer the dimensions automatically.

```
In [4]: model = Sequential()
        model.add(Dense(units=1, input_shape=(2,), activation='sigmoid'))
```

Note that since we are constructing the output layer, and we said it has only one node, the units argument is set to be equal to one. Also, we set the activation equal to sigmoid because the activation function for a Logistic Regression is the logistic function, also called sigmoid in the computer science community.

The neural network is then compiled using the compile function: this declares the optimizer to use and the loss function to minimize. Note that also we can specify the metrics argument, which controls the output metric (for classification problems we set this as accuracy).

```
In [5]: model.compile(optimizer='adam', loss='binary_crossentropy',
                       metrics=['accuracy'])
```

Fitting a model in Keras is pretty straightforward using the method fit on the compiled model. Setting the argument verbose equal to zero means we do not print out the ouput of the model (try by yourself on your local machine if you are interested to see the output), whereas the epochs argument controls the number of times to go over the entire training data. This is a key featrure of deep learning models: when training models we pass through the training data not just once but multiple times!

```
In [6]: fitting = model.fit(x=X, y=y, verbose=0, epochs=50)
        neural_network.plot_loss_accuracy(fitting)

<Figure size 720x432 with 0 Axes>
```

The next snippet generates the decision boundaries produced by the above one-layer neural network. The plot is shown in Figure 4.5.

```
In [7]: neural_network.plot_decision_boundary(lambda x: model.predict(x),X,y)
```

4.2.1 Dealing with Complex Data into a Neural Network

In the previous example we have been working with a datset which was linearly separable. Now we work with non-linear data, and train a logistic regression to see its performance on such dataset.

```
In [8]: X1, y1 = make_circles(n_samples=1000, noise=0.05, factor=0.3,
                              random_state=0)
        neural_network.plot_data(X1,y1)
```

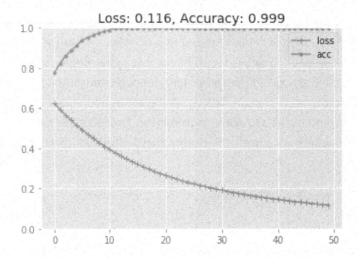

Figure 4.4: Loss vs Accuracy in Fitting a one-layer NN to a linear separable dataset.

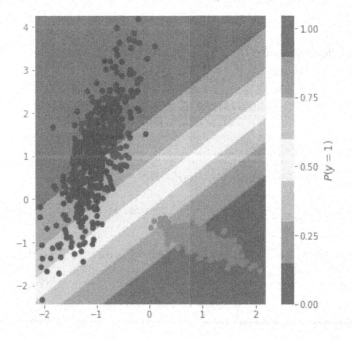

Figure 4.5: Decision Boundaries after fitting a one-layer NN on a linear separable dataset.

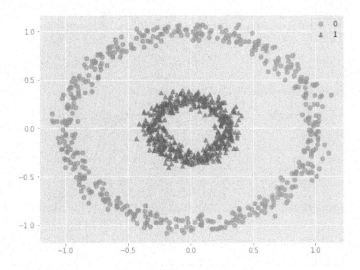

Figure 4.6: Fitting a Logistic Regression on such data would lead to an inconsistent estimator.

Since we want to train a logistic regression model on this new set of data, we proceed as before.

```
In [9]:   model1 = Sequential()
          model1.add(Dense(units=1, input_shape=(2,) , activation='sigmoid'))
          model1.compile(optimizer='adam',loss='binary_crossentropy',
                                          metrics=['accuracy'])
          training1 = model1.fit(x=X1,y=y1,verbose=0, epochs=50)
          y_pred1 = model1.predict_classes(X1, verbose=0)

In [10]:  neural_network.plot_loss_accuracy(training1)

<Figure size 720x432 with 0 Axes>
```

The classifier we have choosen is not a good one, since the accuracy is approximately 50%: this means that wee are missclassifying half of the points, due to the nonlinear behaviour of the dataset.

To fit a neural network on a non-linear dataset, we only need to add more layers to the structure we have just fitted. This is because the output of one layer becomes the input of the next. Keras again does most of the dirty lifting by initializing the weights and biases, and connecting the output of one layer to the input of the next. We only need to specify how many nodes we want in a given layer, and the activation function.

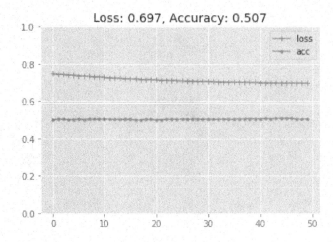

Figure 4.7: Loss vs Accuracy by a one-layer neural network (for different epochs) on a non-linear dataset

```
In [11]: model11 = Sequential()
         model11.add(Dense(units=4,input_shape=(2,),activation='tanh'))
         model11.add(Dense(2, activation='tanh'))
         model11.add(Dense(1, activation='sigmoid'))

         model11.compile(Adam(lr=0.01), loss='binary_crossentropy',
                                       metrics=['accuracy'])
         his = model11.fit(x=X1,y=y1, verbose=0, epochs=100)
         y_pred1 = model1.predict_classes(X1, verbose=0)
```

In practice, we have added a layer with four nodes and tanh activation function. We then add another layer with two nodes again using tanh activation. We finally add the last layer with one single node and sigmoid activation. This is the final layer that we also used in the logistic regression model. This is not a very deep neural network, as it only has three layers: two hidden layers, and the output layer. But notice a couple of patterns:

- Hidden layers use thetanh activation function. If we added more hidden layers, they would also use tanh activation.

- The number of nodes decreases in each subsequent layer. It is good practice to have less nodes as we stack layers on top of one another.

The following snippet produces Figure 4.8, which is shown below.

```
In [12]: neural_network.plot_decision_boundary(
                     lambda x: model11.predict(x), X1, y1)
```

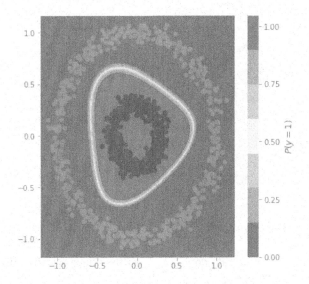

Figure 4.8: Decision boundaries after having fitted a dense neural network with three layers.

4.2.2 Multiclass classification

In the previous sections we worked on binary classification. Now we will take a look at a multi-class classification problem, where the number of classes is more than two. Without loss of generality, we will deal with a three-classes example, but please do note that this approach might be extended to a much greater number of classes.

```
In [13]: X2, y2 = neural_network.make_multiclass(k=3)
```

When dealing with multi-class problems, we use th Softmax Regression, which generalizes the Logistic Regression model with more than two classes. Note that Logistic Regression is used for binary classification problem, and therefore uses a logistic function to get the hard probabilities of classification. However, with Softmax Regression, we use the softmax function: in this case, the classification probabilities are normalized among the classes, which might be weighted. In Keras, for any binary classification problem, we minimize the binary_crossentropy, whereas in the multi-class case, the loss function to minimize is denoted ascategorical_crossentropy. See

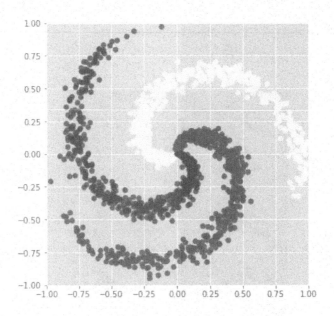

Figure 4.9: Scatter Plot of data concerning a three-class classification problem.

Murphy (2012) for further details on this difference.

Note also that for the fitting phase, in a Softmax Regression the labels need to be in one-hot representation.

```
In [14]: model = Sequential()
         model.add(Dense(output_dim=3,input_shape=(2,),activation='softmax'))
         model.compile('adam','categorical_crossentropy',metrics=['accuracy'])

In [15]: fitting = model.fit(X2, to_categorical(y2), verbose=0, epochs=20)
         neural_network.plot_loss_accuracy(fitting)
         neural_network.plot_multiclass_decision_boundary(model, X2, y2)
```

Obviously, there are important differences between a binary Logistic Regression and a multiclass Softmax Regression. Even fitting a simple Softmax Regression to such data, the performances are not good enough, suggesting that a more dense neural network is required.

```
In [16]: y_pred = model.predict_classes(X2, verbose=0)
         print(classification_report(y2, y_pred))

                 precision    recall  f1-score   support
```

0.0	0.42	0.31	0.36	500
1.0	0.55	0.67	0.60	500
2.0	0.53	0.55	0.54	500
accuracy			0.51	1500
macro avg	0.50	0.51	0.50	1500
weighted avg	0.50	0.51	0.50	1500

Likewise, let us build a deep Artificial Neural Network (ANN) for multiclass classification. To do so, we only need to add more Dense layers, as we did in the previous section. In this example, we add just a couple of Dense layers with tanh activation function.

```
In [18]: model = Sequential()
         model.add(Dense(64, input_shape=(2,), activation='tanh'))
         model.add(Dense(32, activation='tanh'))
         model.add(Dense(16, activation='tanh'))
         model.add(Dense(3, activation='softmax'))

         model.compile('adam', 'categorical_crossentropy',
                              metrics=['accuracy'])

         y_cat = to_categorical(y2)
         history = model.fit(X2, y_cat, verbose=0, epochs=50)
```

Figure 4.11 shows the performances of this model, in terms of confusion matrix: the result is quite remarkable, with an accuracy of approximately 99%!

```
In [19]: neural_network.plot_multiclass_decision_boundary(model, X2, y2)
         y_pred2 = model.predict_classes(X2, verbose=0)
         neural_network.plot_confusion_matrix(model,y2,y_pred2)
```

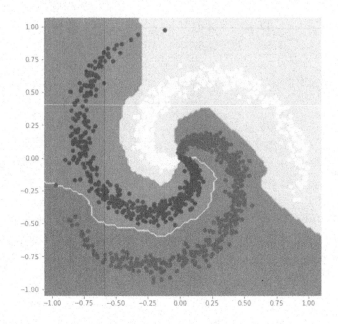

Figure 4.10: Decision Boundaries on a three-class problem produced by a dense neural network.

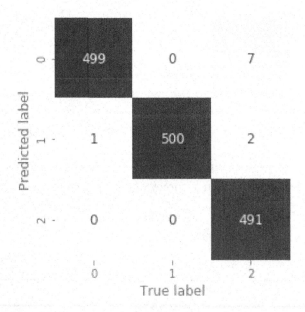

Figure 4.11: Confusion Matrix for a three-class classification problem produced by a dense neural network.

Appendices

Appendix A

A crash course in Python

A concise guide on programming skills in Python is here proposed. The objective is twofold: on the one hand, we will briefly cover all the fundamental building blocks that are strictly necesssary to fully appreciate the algorithms proposed in this book. Indeed, at the end of this appendix, the reader is expected to have gained a solid knowledge and understanding of the Python language, which is indeed a crucial asset if one aims to develop her own model.

On the other hand, the book is based on a book-specific library, called egeaML, available on the GitHub book-specific repository. It consists of a series of methods, used throughout the book, and hence it is important to get into the fundamentals block of Object-Oriented Programming: its understanding, I believe, is absolutely important not only for anyone who wants to deepen his knowledge in Computer Programming, but also for any modern machine learning scientist and engineer who wants to develop analytical softwares.

A.1 Building Blocks in Python

A.1.1 Variables

The most basic building block in Python is the variable: a variable is essentially a box that we can stick a name on, and then we can refer back to it anywhere else in the file. For example, we can create a box, call it a, and assign the integer 5 to it. What we are doing here is just creating a box with the name a and putting the value 5 into it.

```
In [1]: a=5
```

We can, for instance, create a new variable, called my_sum, which simply adds 56 to the variable a, as follows:

```
In [2]: my_sum=a+56
```

Note that variable names could contain letters, special caracters like underscore, and numbers. But be careful: some characters cannot be placed as initializer of your variable. For instance, numbers cannot appear at the beginning of the variable name, as well as amperstand or dollar signs are not allowed. We can also define variables defined as strings, such as

```
In [3]: string_var = 'My name is'
```

```
In [4]: name = 'Bob'
```

Firstly, note that strings are enclosed in quotes. For Python, that word is just a set of characters, and it does not know this is a proper word; it just knows that this is a six-length characters element. We can also print these things out, with the print method, which will print out the value of my variable to the console

```
In [5]: print(string_var + ": " + name )
```

```
My name is: Bob
```

A print is a method, it is just an action, different from the variable. While a variable defines a piece of data, the method on that variable just perfom an action on that piece of data: in this case, print shows on the console the variable we inserted as input. Luckily, the print method is not the only method available in Python.
Note that in order to define a string, we can indistinguishingly use either double or single quote, but sometimes we need to use them togetherself, like as follows:

```
In [6]: sentence_1 = "He told me 'Would you like a coffe?'"
```

```
In [7]: print(sentence_1)
```

By dealing with the print method, it should be now clear that a method always refers to an action (i.e. the print method *prints* something out to the console). The aim of this section is to show other methods, such as the input method, and then showing how to create your own method. If your software could only use the print method, you would probably get very bored, wouldn't you?

A.1.2   Methods

The Input Method

The input method is a built-in function that allows the system to ask iteratively a set of questions to the software user. They are used, for instance, in chatbots, where the user inserts some information to access to a specific functionality. More specifically, the input method prints out into the console a message, and the user is then require to enter some information to get to the next message (or possibly to the desired output).

```
In [8]: num1 = int(input('Please enter an integer value: '))
        num2 = int(input('Please enter another integer value: '))
        print(num1, '+', num2, '=', num1 + num2)

Please enter an integer value: 10
Please enter another integer value: 30
10 + 30 = 40
```

Creating you own method

Before jumping into the methods, let's introduce another fundamental building block in Python: the def keyword. Such a built-in keyword is used to define user-defined functions, and therefore can be exploited to construct our own method.
The definition of our own method requires (at least) basically three components:

- the function header, which begins with the keyword def, and contains the method name;

- the main body, whoch contains the instruction run by the method;

- the return keywork, in case we would like to have a productive function, or a print in case we would be interested in a void function.

See the book *Learning Python - Vol 1* by Clerici et al. (2019) for further details. Note that the main body might also contain docstring, which serves as a function documentation, i.e. describes what the function does, and then there is the actual code performing what the function does.
In the next code, a function that computes the square of a real number is proposed.

```
In [9]: def square(x):
            """ This function returns the square of x"""
            new_value = x ** 2
            return new_value
```

```
In [10]: square(2)
```

```
Out[10]: 4
```

The String Format Method

This method is very useful is ones aim to concatenate variables within a string through positional formatting.

```
In [11]:n = "Bob"
         t = "8 p.m."
         print("Hello {}!! Are we gonna meet at {}?".format(n,t))
```

```
Hello Bob!! Are we gonna meet at 8 p.m.?
```

A.2   Data Structure in Python

A.2.1   List and Tuples

We have discussed about variables, but what we have noticed is that we were creating a variable for every value! This could be a problem: say you have a large number of variables that describe the grades one has gotten at the exams. A student could have many grades, for instance

```
In [12]:grade_1 = 26
         grade_2 = 27
         grade_3 = 28
```

and you want to compute the average grade of a student. We know that an average is the sum of the elements divided by the number of elements in the sample. This translates in Python as follows:

```
In [13]:print((grade_1+grade_2+grade_3)/3)
```

```
27.0
```

Now suppose that a new session comes out, a you take a new exam

```
In [14]:grade_4 =28
         print((grade_1+grade_2+grade_3+grade_4)/4)
```

27.25

but this is not really sustainable. Ideally, what we would have is a way to keep adding grades without the need of creating more varaibles. Luckily, this is possible in Python, using what is called a list. A list is a container of objects, that has the property of being mutable and iterable.

```
In [15]:grades = [26,27,28,28]
         average_grades = sum(grades)/len(grades)
         print(average_grades)
```

27.25

What does this practically mean? In this way we have a very dynamic way to compute the average. Lists therefore allow one not only to write a better and cleaner code, but also to speed up the data analysis process.

However, there are also what are called tuples. Tuples differ from the list in the sense they are immutable, we cannot increase the size of a tuple!!

```
In [16]: tuple_grade = (26,27,28,28) #immutable
```

We could obviously increase the size of a tuple from the beginning, but there are ways for our code to increase the size of grades. For instance, lists can be mutated by using the append method: with that, we are able to increase the size of a list, as follows

```
In [17]: grades.append(29)
         grades
```

```
Out[17]: [26, 27, 28, 28, 29, 29]
```

However, there is no way to increase the size of a tuple, becuase they are immutable! Obvioulsly, tuples can be made dynamic with a little trick:

```
In [18]: tuple_grade = tuple_grade + (29,)
```

```
In [19]:  (26,27,28)+(28,)
```

```
Out[19]:  (26, 27, 28, 28)
```

We haven't changed the tuple! What we have done is just adding to the tuple a new tuple, and creating a new object. Note that the comma is necesasary, otherwise Python is going to read it as a number, but instead should be considered as a tuple.

A.2.2 Sets

You could also have a set of grades: this set is a collection of unique and unordered items. In principle, you could have repeated items inside the set but once you print them, only unique values will be shown. This implies having unordered features, in the sense that the output we get from a print method is completely random; this is not true for lists, where the first element will always appear at the beginning once printed.

```
In [20]:set_grades= {26,27,28,28,21}
```

```
In [21]:print(set_grades)
```

```
{26, 27, 28, 21}
```

For sets, we can add elements witht the add method

```
In [22]:  set_grades.add(30)
          print(set_grades)
```

```
{26, 27, 28, 30}
```

A.2.3 Dictionaries

Dictionaries are a sort of list but with a very nice property, which we will se in a few moments. They are not tuples, since they are mutable, and they have something similar to an order, so they cannot be considered as a proper generlization of the sets, even because, by structure, multiple identical items are allowed in dictionaries.

We can note that none of the previous data structure were able to index each specific element. In other words, we would love having a key for each element in that set, that is a description for each value shown in the dictionary. This is done in Python using dictionaries, which are defined as a key-value set.

Without loss of generality, we now show a Dictionary with two key, say names that correspond to students, and their corresponding grade in Computere science exam. In particular, those values are given in terms of lists.

```
In [23]:my_dict = {'name':['Bob','Frank','Maria'],
                    'grades':[26,27,28]}
```

The elements are still unordered but now they are in their own anymore, they are separated by a semicolon and there is a relationship between the key and the value: thanks to this relationship we are able to store data. Dictionaries are mutable, and we can therefore modify their structure. In general, if we want to access to keys, we have to do as follows:

```
In [24]:my_dict['name']
```

```
Out[24]: ['Bob', 'Frank', 'Maria']
```

We can add new values to the given keys, as follows

```
In [25]:my_dict['students'].append('Anna')
        my_dict['grades'].append(28)
```

Coming back to the list average example, where we have computed the average score from a list of exam scores, we now compute the same quantity from a dictionary

```
In [26]: float(format(sum(my_new_dict['grades'])/4,'.2f'))
```

```
Out[26]: 27.25
```

A.3 Loops in Python

A.3.1 The For Loop

In any programming language, loops are very useful iterative structures to execute several times the same task. The simplest logic for writing a loop is illustrated by the following example, which prints out the integers from 0 through 6, included:

```
In [27]:my_list = []
        for c in range(7):
            my_list.append(c)
        print(my_list)
```

```
[0,1,2,3,4,5,6]
```

Another example is the following one: we are going to create a new list, called squared, which takes the square of the 1-dim vector my_list element-wise.

```
In [28]:my_list = [1,2,3,5,6,9]
         squared = []
         for i in my_list:
             a = i**2
             squared.append(a)
         print(squared)
```

```
[1, 4, 9, 25, 36, 81]
```

A.3.2   The While Loop

While the for loop is a loop based on a counter, the while one is based essentially on a condition. In particular, a while loop os made up two parts:

1. The while clause with a condition, of which the true or false value occur;

2. A body that is repeated until the condition is False

Note that a while loop requires an exit condition, otherwise the iterative structure defined as such is going to be run forever and ever! As an illustration, we write a program that asks to insert some information regarding a client; the request stop whenever the user correctly insert them.

```
In [29]:while True:
             int(input("Enter the user bank account number "))
             input("Enter his name: ")
             input("Enter the password: ")
             keep_going = input("Continue? (y/n)").lower()
             if keep_going == 'n':
                 break
```

```
Enter the user bank account number 3465123
Enter his name: Bob
Enter the password: abracadabra
Continue? (y/n) n
```

A.4 Advanced Data Structure in Python

A.4.1 List comprehensions

So far we have used lists, as the one given below, which shows integrs from zero to four.

```
In [30]:my_list = [0,1,2,3,4]
```

We can get the same result using the so-called list comprehension, which is a particular way to write an interative structure in Python - we say that list comprehensions are the Pythonic way of writing a for loop.

```
In [31]:my_py_list = [n for n in range(5)]
```

Well, let's try to understand its logic behind the hood. Basically, it is a for loop, and n is going to be the first element of that loop, which is then stored into a list by enclosing everything in square brackets, that is it tells python to put n in a list. It is basically a for loop, as the following one:

```
In [32]:def my_list(num):
            """Returns a list of integer numbers from a range"""
            my_list = []
            for n in range(num):
                my_list.append(n)
            return my_list
        my_list(5)
```

```
Out[32]: [0, 1, 2, 3, 4]
```

Hence, we can enclose in a list comprehesion any object (or any action or instruction) we could think of. Take, for instance, the square function (we saw in Section A.1) and apply it to a range of number:

```
In [33]:def power(num, power=2):
            """Returns the square of a list of values.
            We could also change the power of the function."""
            squared_list = []
            for n in range(num):
                val = n**power
                squared_list.append(val)
```

```
        return squared_list


    power(5)
```

Out[33]: [0, 1, 4, 9, 16]

The same thing can be written in terms of list comprehensions.

```
In [34]:squared_list = [x**2 for x in range(5)]
        print(squared_list)
```

[0, 1, 4, 9, 16]

We have gotten each element of the iterable squared! Now we are going to see how to add conditions within a list comprehension. For instance, we would like to return a list that takes, from the range(10), just the even numbers or better the numbers with remainder equal to zero whenever divided by two.

```
In [35]:evens = [n for n in range(10+1) if n%2==0]
        evens
```

Out[35]: [0, 2, 4, 6, 8, 10]

Equivalently, using our own method even(), we get the same result:

```
In [36]: def even():
            num = int(input("Enter a number: "))
            evens = []
            for n in range(num+1):
                if n%2==0:
                    evens.append(n)
            return evens
        even()
```

Enter a number: 10

Out[36]: [0, 2, 4, 6, 8, 10]

A.4.2   Lambda Functions

Let us consider the following list of integers:

```
In [37]: nums = [48,6,9,21,3]
```

We would like to create a function that squares that number. How can we do that? We might create our method, as we did before:

```
In [38]:def square(nums):
            square = []
            for x in nums:
                square.append(x**2)
            return square
        square(nums)
```

```
Out[38]: [2304, 36, 81, 441, 9]
```

Alternatively, we can use the so-called *anonymous functions*, which in Python refer to the lambda functions: they are not just pythonist, but they are used in other languages, such as Java.

```
In [39]:(lambda x: x**2, nums)
```

```
Out[39]:(<function __main__.<lambda>(x)>, [48, 6, 9, 21, 3])
```

We have created a new function, a lambda function, that applies to the list nums. But how can I unpack the results from my function? Well, anonymous functions are unpacked with the map() function. Map is going to apply the square() function to each element of the list vector. However, note that the map() itself is not sufficient to unpack the lambda. We must call the list() method to see the result.

```
In [40]:list(map(lambda x: x**2, nums))
```

```
Out[40]:[2304, 36, 81, 441, 9]
```

We close the section with another example using lambda functions. However, differently from before, we are not going to apply the map() to each single element; instead, we are going to filter out all the members of the list that do not satisfy the requirement. In this case, we are going to ask the user a number, and then checking its proper divisors, which are going to be stored in another list.

```
In [41]: num = int(input("number: "))
         divisors = []
         for n in range(2,num):
             if num%n ==0:
                 divisors.append(n)
             else:
                 pass
         print(divisors)
```

```
number: 12
[2,3,4,6]
```

```
In [42]:print(list(filter(lambda x: num%x==0, range(2,num))))
```

```
Out[42]:[2,3,4,6]
```

A.5   Advanced Concepts on Functions

A.5.1   The magic of Wildcards into Function's arguments

This section aims at answering to a simple question: How can we deal with multiple and unforseen arguments inside a function?

Flexible Arguments

Suppose you want to write a function but you don't know how many arguments the function requires. Take for instance the following example:

```
In [43]:def average_grades(e1,e2,e3):
             return (e1+e2+e3)/3

         print(average_grades(28,26,24))
```

```
26.0
```

But then you take more exams, and so you have to take care of the denominator and the arguments in the sum! Luckily, in Python we have a smartest way to do that, and that is with flexible arguments, called args.

```
In [44]:def average_grades_flex(*args):
            tot_exams = 0
            for n in args:
                tot_exams +=1
            return sum(args)/tot_exams

        print(average_grades_flex(28,26,24))
```

26.0

Flexible Keyword Arguments

Typically, we refer to args if one wants to use non-keyworded variables inside the function. But what about having to deal with keyworded arguments? In that case, we use the *kwargs argument, which allows you to handle named arguments in a function. To understand what kwargs are, let us consider the following example.

```
In [45]:def what_are_kwargs(*args, **kwargs):
            print(args)
            print(kwargs)

        what_are_kwargs(10,20,30)
```

(10, 20, 30)
{}

We see that we have gotten an empty dictionary. This should not come as surprise. Indeed, kwargs are used for keyworded arguments, and therefore are structured, by default, as a key-value object. If, for instance, we add two keyworded arguments, such as name and job, we now see they appear in the initializded dictionary.

```
In [46]: what_are_kwargs(10,20,30, name='James', job='Teacher' )
```

(10, 20, 30)
{'name': 'James', 'job': 'Teacher'}

Example: Total Monthly Wage

Let's see a practical example to better understand this concept.

```
In [47]:def total_wage(pay_hour,hours,working_days):
            """ Returns the monthly wage"""
            val = hours*pay_hour*working_days
            return val


        print("I have earned a gross salary of €",
                          format(total_wage(25,8,22),'.2f'))

I have earned a gross salary of € 4400.00
```

That function is fine, since it computes the monthly gross salary, but we are not taking into account extra worked hours, or even taxes!

```
In [48]: def taxes():
             """ Returns the taxes to be paid, based on the wage"""
             monthly_income = float(input("How much do you earn? "))
             taxes = 0
             if monthly_income <= 1500:
                 taxes = 0
             elif monthly_income <= 2400:
                 taxes = monthly_income*0.15
             elif monthly_income <= 3800:
                 taxes = monthly_income*0.25
             elif monthly_income <= 4900:
                 taxes = monthly_income*0.3
             else:
                 taxes = monthly_income*0.5
             return taxes


         def total_wage_full(pay_hour,hours,working_days,
                             extra_hours,extra_pay,taxes):
             """ It returns the net monthly wage"""
             val = hours*pay_hour*working_days +
                         extra_hours*extra_pay -taxes
             return val
```

In [49]: print("I have earned a net salary of €",
            format(total_wage_full(25,8,22,10,29,taxes()),'.2f'))

How much do you earn? 4400
I have earned a net salary of € 3370.00

Luckily in Python we have a very dynamic and flexible way to do that: use the keyword *args!

In [50]: def total_wage_full(pay_hour,hours, working_days,*args):
            val = hours*pay_hour*working_days +
                        args[0]*args[1] - args[2]
            return val

In [51]: print("I have earned a net salary of €",
            format(total_wage_full(25,8,22,10,29,taxes()),'.2f'))

How much do you earn? 4400
I have earned a net salary of € 3370.00

Suppose we want to add also the employee name, job title and fiscal year to that list. In order to add keyword arguments in a flexible manner, ther is the keyword *kwargs, which replicates the *args keyword in its syntax.

In [52]: def total_wage(pay_hour,hours,working_days,*args,**kwargs):
            val = format(hours*pay_hour*working_days +
                    args[0]*args[1] - args[2], '.2f')
            message = "{} has earned a net salary of € {}
                        with her job of {} in {}."
                    .format(kwargs['name'],val,
                    kwargs['job'],kwargs['year'])
            return message

        print(total_wage(25,8,22,10,29,taxes(),
                    name='James', job='Teacher',year='2018'))

How much do you earn? 4400
James has earned a net salary of € 3370.00 with her job of
Teacher in 2018.

A.5.2   Local vs Global Scope in Functions

We go into what is called the scope in functions: not all objects are accessible every-where in a script. To begin with, we have two main scope:

- Global Scope: defined in the main body of a script;

- Local Scope: defined inside a Function;

- Built-in-scope: names in the predefined builtins module.

Local scope means that once the execution of the function is done, any name inside it cease to exist, and you cannot access to them anymore. In the next snippet, the variable new_value is defined locally, and hence if it is called outside, the user will get an error.

```
In [53]:def square(x):
            """ This function returns the square of x"""
            new_value = x ** 2
            return new_value
        new_value
```

Suppose now we have the same function as before but now, instead, the variable is defined outside the function. This is a global variable, since it can be recalled anywhere in the script.

```
In [54]:new_value = 10
        def square(x):
            """ This function returns the square of x"""
            new_value2 = new_value ** 2
            return new_value2
        square(3)
```

```
Out[54]: 100
```

Note that if the value is not internally defined, then we look for global values (the other way round does not apply). To recap, when we reference a name, first local scope is searched, then the global; if the name is in neither, then the built-in scope is searched. Please check the book of Lutz (2013) for further details on this topic.

The Global Keyword

We can tell Python to use a global variable inside a method by using the keyword global: in this case, Python is looking for the variable outside the method, and use it. Furthermore, it can also be updated, since the local variable is now the global one, as follows:

```
In [55]: new_value = 10
         def square(x):
             """ This function returns the square of x"""
             global new_value
             new_value = new_value ** 2
             return new_value
         square(3)

Out[55]: 100

In [56]: print(new_value)

100
```

A.6   Introduction to Object-Oriented Programming

To fully appreciate the importance of this topic, let's first understand why we need Object-Oriented Programming (OOP). In general, data analytics softwares are very complex programs, which are defined as a sequence of instructions that manipulate data in a meaningful way. As an example, suppose we want to create a program that computes the average grade of a Student. We could, for instance, write the following:

```
In [57]: grades = input("Tell me your grades,
                         separated by commas: ").split(',')

         def average_grades(grades):
             tot = 0
             for n in range(len(grades)):
                 grades[n] = int(grades[n])
                 tot +=grades[n]
```

```
avg = format(tot/len(grades), '.2f')
return avg
```

```
print(average_grades(grades))
```

```
Tell me your grades, separated by commas: 26,27,29
27.33
```

But now the question is: how do we manage the building procedure of a more complex software? Suppose that we are not just interested in computing the average grade of a Student, but we also want to store her personal information, like age, name, surname, gender, and so on, possibly repeating it infinitely-many times. How do we accomplish this task? In other words, if you want to represent a person, with some features, none of the built-in functions would allow to do that. In Python, we make use of the OOP paradigm: we can say that OOP is a methodology that allows to design and develop large software projects easier and more intuitively.

A.6.1   Objects, Classes and Attributes

In general, a program is made by different objects. In Python, we have many kind of objects. We have sequences (like strings, lists and tuples), dictionaries, methods but even variables. More precisely, we can say that an object is characterized by a type, some attributes and some methods, that allow to manipulate and use the object itself.

In Python, to create an object we use classes: they define a type object, and from a single class we can create many unique objects, which will share some common characteristics, but they are uniquely identified by the values assigned to the attributes of the class! A class notably tells python how an object should be defined, but it does not actually create it. The process of creating an object from a class is called instantiation, which means taking a class, and creating an object from it with specific attributes. We can say that attributes make unique each object, and they can be changed without affecting the attributes of other objects created from the same class. But *how do we create a class*? We use the keyword class followed by the class name; everything after the colon will be indented into the class, and it will be specific to that class.

```
In [58]:class Student:
            pass
```

But we all know that a student has specific characteristics, like name, age, school, and so on. Hence, we assign them to the class by using the init method: it is called initializer because whenever an object is created, its attributes automatically get the default value given in the init method. Note that we have to include the self parameter so that our initializer has a reference to the new object being initialised, which basically plays the role of connector beetween objects inside the class.

```
In [59]:class Student:
            def __init__(self,name,age,school):
                self.name = name
                self.age = age
                self.school = school
                self.marks = []

            def average(self):
                return round(sum(self.marks)/len(self.marks),2)

        student = Student("James",20,"MIT")
        student.marks.append(26)
        student.marks.append(27)
        student.marks.append(29)
        print(student.average())
```

27.33

Let's give some comments to the previous chunk of code. First of all, note that an instance of the class Student was created by giving some attributes to it, e.g. Student("James",20,"MIT").

Secondly, we have added a productive method called average, which computes the average grade of that student. Defining methods inside classes is very important, because they make the classes dynamic and useful. This example basically replicates the one we saw at the beginning of this tutorial, but it is more readable and easier to understand, isn't it?

Last but not least, we can access to each attribute of that instance as follows

```
In [60]:print(student.name)
        print(student.school)
        print(student.marks)
```

James
MIT
[26, 27, 29]

A.6.2   Subclasses and Inheritance

To introduce this concept, we will focus on a simple example, that describes the students involved in a specific Python classroom. We will therefore create a class object, called PythonSchool, which will contain the people involved (expressed as a list), and a series of objects inside it. In particular, we will discuss about subclasses and inheritance: as for the former, we will create two subclasses, say DataScientist and DataEngineer, which will be strictly dependent on the superclass DataScience, whioch describe the student involved in the Python classroom devoted to Data Science skills. In particolar, when we inherit something, it does not mean cloning, right? So we do as follows: we implement the init method but then, inside it, we call the superclass: DataScience is therefore the super class, and we call its init method in that way, so that we inherit the parameters from the super class also in the subclasses. Then, what happens is that the classes DataScientst and DataEngineer contain everything that the class DataScience contains. Let us see in practice this pipeline: I will comment each step inside the code for a better readibility and explanation.

```
In [61]:class PythonSchool:


         students = []
         #initialization of an empty list of students


         def __init__(self, students):
             self.students = students


     class DataScience:
         # We initialize the superclass,
         # which produces a Description of the Student.
         def __init__(self, name, age, job):
             self.name= name
             self.age=age
             self.job=job
             # This describes the actual job
```

```
        self.language = input("Which high-level language
                             do you use for data science?")


    def Description(self):
        print("This is", self.name, \
              "who has", self.age, "years old", \
              "and earns €", format(int(self.income), ','))


# Here we introduce two subclasses, say DataScientist
# and Data Engineer.

class DataScientist(DataScience):
    def __init__(self,name,age,job,hobby):
        super().__init__(name,age,job)
        self.hobby = hobby
        self.dream = int(input("Which position you would
                               like to apply for? "))



class DataEngineer(DataScience):
    def __init__(self,name,age,job,hobby):
        super().__init__(name,age,job)
        self.hobby = hobby
        self.dream = int(input("Which position you would
                               like to apply for? "))


# We now create instances of students

student_list = [
    DataScientist("Bob",39,"Software Engineer","Running"),
    DataEngineer("Helen",30,"Stack Developer","Cycling"),
    DataScientist("James",46,"Consultant","Phylosophy")
    ]


my_class = DataScience(student_list)

# We now create a list containing the descriptions
```

```
# of the students.

my_list = []
for p in my_class.student:
    t = ["This is", p.name,
         "who is", str(p.age), "years old",
         "and uses the software", p.language,
         "for Data Science as a",p.job,"."\n
         "He loves", p.hobby,
         "and he looking for a poistion of",p.dreams]
    my_sep = ' '
    mess = my_sep.join(t)
    my_list.append(mess)
```

As an advanced in-depth analysis, the interest reader might find on the book-specific GitHub repository a data science application, namely a .ipynb notebook file, which describes on how to structure an advanced project using OOP on the mtcars dataset.

Appendix B

Mathematics behind the skip-gram model

We wish to minimize Equation 4.1 using gradient descent. Hence, we have the following partial derivatives to compute on $\log\left(\frac{e^{u_c^T \cdot v_w}}{\sum_{v \in V} e^{u_v^T \cdot v_w}}\right)$:

$$\frac{\partial}{\partial v_w} \log\left(\frac{e^{u_c^T \cdot v_w}}{\sum_{v \in V} e^{u_v^T \cdot v_w}}\right) = \frac{\partial}{\partial v_w} \log\left(e^{u_c^T \cdot v_w}\right) - \frac{\partial}{\partial v_w} \log\left(\sum_{v \in V} e^{u_v^T \cdot v_w}\right)$$

Let us compute separately the two quantities. The positive term is easy, since we have to compute the following derivative:

$$\frac{\partial}{\partial v_w} \log\left(e^{u_c^T \cdot v_w}\right) = \frac{\partial}{\partial v_w}\left(u_c^T \cdot v_w\right)$$

This translates into the following system:

$$\begin{cases} \frac{\partial}{\partial v_{w1}}\left(u_{01} \cdot v_{w1} + u_{01} \cdot v_{w2} + \ldots + u_{01} \cdot v_{wd}\right) \\ \frac{\partial}{\partial v_{w2}}\left(u_{01} \cdot v_{w1} + u_{01} \cdot v_{w2} + \ldots + u_{01} \cdot v_{wd}\right) \\ \ldots\ldots\ldots \\ \frac{\partial}{\partial v_{wd}}\left(u_{01} \cdot v_{w1} + u_{01} \cdot v_{w2} + \ldots + u_{01} \cdot v_{wd}\right) \end{cases} = \begin{bmatrix} u_{01} \\ u_{02} \\ \vdots \\ u_{0d} \end{bmatrix} = u_0$$

The negative term is more complicated, and we use the chain rule to compute it.

$$\frac{\partial}{\partial v_w} \log \left(\sum_{v \in V} e^{u_v^T \cdot v_w} \right) = \frac{1}{\left(\sum_{v \in V} e^{u_v^T \cdot v_w} \right)} \frac{\partial}{\partial v_w} \left(\sum_{x=1}^{V} e^{u_x^T \cdot v_w} \right)$$

$$= \frac{1}{\left(\sum_{v \in V} e^{u_v^T \cdot v_w} \right)} \cdot \sum_x e^{u_x^T \cdot v_w} \cdot \frac{\partial}{\partial v_w} \left(u_x^T v_w \right)$$

Merging the two quantities, we have that:

$$\frac{\partial}{\partial v_w} \log \left(\frac{e^{u_c^T \cdot v_w}}{\sum_{v \in V} e^{u_v^T \cdot v_w}} \right) = u_0 - \sum_{x=1}^{V} \frac{e^{u_x^T \cdot v_w}}{\left(\sum_{v \in V} e^{u_v^T \cdot v_w} \right)} \cdot u_x$$

$$= u_0 - \sum_{x=1}^{V} p\left(x | w \right) \cdot u_x$$

where u_0 is the observed representation of the context word, and u_x is the expected vector representation of the context, weighted by the probability of each word in the vocabulary. Hence, the negative quantity can be understood as the expected context word according tothe observed vector u.

I leave for the interested reader the exercise to obtain the partial derivatives the loss function with respect to the context words v_c, following the same argument as the one given here.

Index

Accuracy, 80

Cross-validation, 27

Deep Learning
    Keras, 155
    Multi-class Classification, 161

Ensemble, 99
    AdaBoost, 111
    Bagging, 104
    CatBoost, 122
    Gradient Boosting, 112
    Random Forests, 107
    Voting Classifier, 100
    XGBoost, 115

F1-score, 82

Kernelized Support Vector Machine, 91

Linear Models
    Elastic Net, 70
    Huber Regression, 71
    Lasso, 67
    Logistic Regression, 76
    Ordinary Least Square, 60
    RANSAC, 74
    Ridge, 62

Natural Language Processing
    Bag-of-Words, 137

Paragraph Vector Representation, 153
    Preprocessing, 132
    Similarity, 146
    TFIDF, 142
Nearest Neighbor, 18

Precision, 81
Preprocessing
    Box-Cox Transformation, 36
    Categorical Variables, 38
    Imbalanced Dataset, 43
    Missing Values, 41
    Principal Component Analysis, 49
    Scaling, 32
    SMOTE, 47
    t-SNE, 55

Recall, 81

Shap, 117
Skip-gram model, 149
Support Vector Machine, 86

Bibliography

[1] M Abadi et al. TensorFlow: Large-scale machine learning on heterogeneous systems. http://tensorflow.org/, 2015.

[2] Robert Andersen. *Modern Methods for Robust Regression*, volume 152 of *Quantitative Applications in the Social Sciences*. SAGE, 2008.

[3] Y. Bengio, H. Schwenk, J.S. Senecal, F. Morin, and J.L. Gauvain. Neural probabilistic language models. *Innovations in Machine Learning*, pages 137–186, 2006.

[4] S. Bird, E. Loper, and E. Klein. *Natural Language Processing with Python*. O'Reilly Media Inc., 2009.

[5] C.M. Bishop. *Pattern Recognition and Machine Learning*. Springer, 2006.

[6] G.E.P. Box and D.R. Cox. An analysis of transformations. *Journal of the Royal Statistical Society B,*, 26:211–252, 1964.

[7] L. Breiman. Random forests. *Machine Learning*, 45(5–32), 2001.

[8] L. Breiman, J. H. Friedman, R. A. Olshen, and C. J. Stone. *Classification and Regression Trees*. Chapman and Hall/CRC, 1984.

[9] N.V. Chawla, K.W. Bowyer, L.O Hall, and W.P. Kegelmeyer. Smote: Synthetic minority over-sampling technique. *Journal of Artificial Intelligence Research*, 16, 2002.

[10] T. Chen and C. Guestrin. Xgboost: A scalable tree boosting system. *Proceedings of the 22nd ACM SIGKDD International Conference on Knowledge Discovery and Data Mining*, pages 785–794, 2016.

[11] F. Chollet. *Deep Learning with Python*. Manning Publications, 2017.

[12] F. Chollet et al. Keras. https://keras.io, 2015.

[13] A. Clerici, M. de Pra, M.C. Debernardi, and D. Tosi. *Learning Python*. Pixel. EGEA, 2019.

[14] A.C. Courville, I. Goodfellow, and Y. Bengio. *Deep Learning*. MIT, 2017.

[15] H.T. Fanaee and J. Gama. Event labeling combining ensemble detectors and background knowledge. *J. Prog Artif Intell*, 2:113–127, 2014.

[16] M.A. Fischler and R.C. Bolles. RANdom SAmple Consensus: a paradigm for model fitting with applications to image analysis and automated cartography. *Communications of the ACM*, 26(6):381–395, 1981.

[17] R. A. Fisher. On the mathematical foundations of theoretical statistics. *Philos. Trans. Roy. Soc. London Ser. A*, 222(309-368), 1922.

[18] Y. Freund and R.E. Schapire. Experiments with a new boosting algorithm. In *Machine Learning: Proceedings of the Thirteenth International Conference*, pages 148–156. Morgan Kaufmann, 1996.

[19] J. Friedman, R. Tibshirani, and T. Hastie. *The Elements of Statistical Learning*. Springer, 2008.

[20] J.H. Friedman. Greedy function approximation: A gradient boosting machine. *Annals of Statistics*, 29(5):1189–1232, 2001.

[21] X. Glorot, A. Bordes, and Y. Bengio. Domain adaptation for large-scale senti-ment classi- fication: A deep learning approach. In *Proceedings of the 26th International Conference on Machine Learning (ICML)*, pages 513–520, 2011.

[22] Z. Harris. Distributional structure. *Word*, 1954.

[23] G.E. Hinton, J.L. McClelland, and D.E. Rumelhart. *Distributed representations. In: Parallel distributed processing: Explorations in the microstructure of cognition*, volume Volume 1: Foundations. MIT Press, 1986.

[24] P.J. Huber. Robust Estimation of a Location Parameter. *Ann. Math. Statist.*, 35 (1):73–101, 1964.

[25] O. Levy and Y. Goldberg. Dependency-based word embeddings. In *Volume: Proceedings of the 52nd Annual Meeting of the Association for Computational Linguistics (Volume 2: Short Papers)*, 2014.

[26] S.M. Lundeber and Su-In Lee. A unified approach to interpreting model predictions. In *Advances in Neural Information Processing Systems 30 (NIPS 2017)*, 2017.

[27] M. Lutz. *Learning Python*. O'Reilly Media Inc., 2013.

[28] A.L. Maas, R.E. Daly, P.T. Pham, D. Huang, A.Y. Ng, and C. Potts. Learning word vectors for sentiment analysis. *Proceedings of the 49th Annual Meeting of the Association for Computational Linguistics.*, 2011.

[29] C.D. Manning, P. Raghavan, and H. Schutze. *Introduction to Information Retrieval*. Cambridge University Press, 2008.

[30] T. Mikolov and Q. Le. Distributed representations of sentences and documents. In *Proceedings of the 31st International Conference on Machine Learning*, volume 32, pages 1188–1196, 2014.

[31] T. Mikolov, K. Chen, G. Corrado, and J. Dean. Efficient estimation of word representations in vector space. In *ICLR Workshop*, 2013.

[32] T. Mikolov, I. Sutskever, K. Chen, G. Corrado, and J. Dean. Distributed representations of words and phrases and their compositionality. In *Advances in Neural Information Processing Systems*, 2013.

[33] A.C. Muller and S. Guido. *Introduction to Machine Learning with Python*. O'Reilly Media Inc, 2017.

[34] K. Murphy. *Machine Learning: a Probabilistc Perspective*. MIT Press, 2012.

[35] F. Pedregosa, G. Varoquaux, A. Gramfort, V. Michel, B. Thirion, O. Grisel, M. Blondel, P. Prettenhofer, R. Weiss, V. Dubourg, J. Vanderplas, A. Passos, D. Cournapeau, M. Brucher, M. Perrot, and E. Duchesnay. Scikit-learn: Machine learning in python. *Journal of Machine Learning Research*, 12:2825–2830, 2011.

[36] J. Pennington, R. Socher, and C.D. Manning. Glove: Global vectors for word representation. 2014.

[37] M. Porter. An algorithm for suffix stripping. *Program*, 14(3):130–137, 1980.

[38] L. Prokhorenkova, G. Gusev, A. Vorobev, A.V. Dorogush, and A. Gulin. Catboost: unbiased boosting with categorical features. *NeurIPS2018*, 2018.

[39] L.S. Shapley. A value for n-person games. *Contributions to the Theory of Games*, 2 (28):307–317., 1953.

[40] R Socher, C.L. Cliff, A.Y Ng, and C.D. Manning. Parsing natural scenes and natural language with recursive neural networks. volume 2, 2011.

[41] R. Tibshirani. Regression shrinkage and selection via the lasso. *Journal of the Royal Statistical Society B*, 58(1):267–288, 1996.

[42] R. Tibshirani. The lasso problem and uniqueness. *Electronic Journal of Statistics*, 7:1456–1490, 2013.

[43] L.P.J. van der Maaten and G.E. Hinton. Visualizing data using t-sne. *Journal of Machine Learning Research*, 9:2579–2605, 2008.

[44] J. Vanderplas. *Python Data Science Handbook*. O'Reilly Media Inc., 2016.

[45] I.K. Yeo and R.A. Johnson. A new family of power transformations to improve normality or symmetry. *Biometrika*, 87(4):954–959, 2000.

[46] H. Zou and T. Hastie. Regularization and variable selection via the elastic net. *Journal of the Royal Statistical Society B*, 67:301–320, 2005.

[47] N. Zumel and J. Mount. *Practical Data Science with R*. Manning Publications, 2014.